MAKING SUNDAY

SUNDAY

Special

Karen Burton
Mains

WORD BOOKS
PUBLISHER
WACO, TEXAS

A DIVISION OF
WORD, INCORPORATED

MAKING SUNDAY SPECIAL

Library of Congress Cataloging-in-Publication Data

Mains, Karen Burton.
  Making Sunday special.

  1. Sunday. I. Title.
BV111.M27 1987   263'.4   86–32576
ISBN 0–8499–0612–1
ISBN 0–8499–3079–0 (paperback)

Printed in the United States of America

7898 BKC 987654321

To the men and women
who have given their lives
to making Sunday holy.
May we together
rebuild the walls that have been
torn down.

Contents

A Short Word of Explanation   9

Part I. The High Point of the Week
    (How to Make Sunday the Best Day)   11

  1. Making Sunday Special   13
  2. Jewish Sabbath Tradition   25
  3. Lord's Day Eve   39
  4. Lord's Day Preparations   53
  5. Getting Organized   65
  6. Getting Rid of Sunday Anxieties   75
  7. Getting Heart and Mind Ready   87
  8. Getting-Started Exercises   97
  9. The Sacred Rhythm of Work and Play   113
10. Lord's Day Participation   125
11. Making Time Holy   137

Part II. The Heart of a Sabbath Keeper
    (Why Love Makes Sunday Special)   147

12. The Gentleman Caller   149
13. The Ring   159
14. Mental Fidelity   169
15. The Bridal Procession   181

A Short Word
of Explanation

After twenty-five years of marriage, a working team of husband and wife reaches a juncture where it is sometimes impossible to distinguish one's vision and the other's calling. This has happened to David and myself; I often don't know where his work leaves off and mine begins. It is only in a good working marriage that mates can plagiarize one another outrageously without causing upset.

Much of the heartbeat behind *Making Sunday Special* reflects the initiative and concern of my husband, David R. Mains. Certainly, the pragmatic helps, charts, and practical responses are his creative children. Our personal journey into making Sunday the high point of the week is a corporate undertaking that has occurred over a twenty-year period. Although my name is the byline on this project and I have done the actual writing, the book could not have been conceived without David's experimentation and theological comprehension. A lovely development in our relationship is that neither one of us cares who of us gets the credit.

Much of the material has been tested within the listening audience of the Chapel of the Air, a daily religious broadcast that is aired over some five hundred outlets in the United States. These listeners have proven a willing laboratory for our ideas, testing concepts and responding to their effect through their mail comments. David and I feel strongly that Sunday is so dangerously secularized

among Christians that we have dedicated our Saturday
broadcasts to helping our audience get ready for church
the next day. Consequently, thousands of individual participants and hundreds of churches have provided valu-
able feedback as to the efficacy of these ideas. Most are
experiencing a Sunday attitude reformation. Sunday is,
once again, becoming the best day of the week.

This book is divided into two sections. Part One is an
examination of the contemporary approach to Sunday
(Why is it often the worst day of the week? What did
God intend it to be? And how do we make it special?)
This section is filled with practical helps to revolutionize
Sunday observance.

Part Two is more theoretical, developing a motif in
Scripture, God's love motif, without which the Sunday
observance degenerates into legalism which eventually
chokes the beauty out of the Lord's Day experience.
When the pendulum swings into law alone, reactionism
is sure to follow on the upward stroke, which is exactly
what has occurred in our contemporary generation. *Experiencing* God's love rationale is what regenerates our
Sunday remembrance. This book hopes to restore Sunday reality with renewal concepts which have been lost
to at least three generations, maybe more.

The terms *Shabbat, Sabbath,* and *Sabbath/Sunday* are
not used interchangeably in the book. *Shabbat* refers to
Old Testament, Jewish observance. *Sabbath* refers to contemporary Jewish tradition and practice. *Sabbath/Sunday*
refers to the attitude and inclination which we Christians
should bring to our Lord's Day observance. We must learn
how to observe Sunday with a Sabbath understanding.

Excerpts from *The Jewish Catalog* (edited by Richard
Siegel, Michael Strassfeld, and Sharon Strassfeld) refer
to the Jewish tradition of Shabbat which is observed
from Friday sundown until Saturday sundown.

May Christ be Lord again of all our Sabbaths. May we
truly learn to make Sunday special.

PART I

THE
HIGH
POINT
OF THE
WEEK

How to Make Sunday the Best Day

1

Making Sunday Special

MY PARENTS BOUGHT an old house in Wheaton, Illinois, because Mother loved the elms which leaned together, their boughs touching in greeting, the sidewalk and lawn shadowed beneath their leafy canopy. I was eight years old when we moved to this house from the city, from Logan Boulevard and Brentano School and Lincoln Park along Lake Michigan to the suburb with its shading elms edged by cornfields and its public schools named after New England poets—Lowell, Longfellow, Whittier, Holmes, Emerson.

The house was over one hundred years old, a wonderful age it seemed to me then, and was constructed with remarkable incongruities. Floors angled out and downward from the center of each room so that marbles rolled to the corners. The upstairs bedroom in which we children slept was unheated, and on winter mornings we rolled reluctantly from beneath the maroon down

13

comforter and gingerly padded across the cold, cracked linoleum. None of the closets had doors; but fabric curtains, hung from sagging string, hid the disorder of shoes, bargain-basement buys, second-hand suits, and homemade clothes made over from outgrown garments, the fabric turned to hide wool-wear, the lining and buttons new.

A magnanimous monster ruled the dank basement, a coal-burning furnace with uplifted hot air vents like round outstretched fat woman's arms. Into the flame of its hungry belly we fed shovels-full of shining black chunks of fuel. The coal truck latched its umbilical chute and with a rumbling, tumbling downward sound filled the bin with our allotted winter's solace. On cold, dark mornings, the thermostat low and sinking, I watched as my father took huge tongs and extracted clinkers from the ashes in the furnace, discarding them in garden baskets. He stoked the fire, it roared to life; and together we slammed shut the gray metal door, pushing the end of the latch up with firm fists. Then we climbed the cellar stairs in the light of a dim solitary bulb, past the round fieldstones set in crumbling cement, past the rows of glass jars—grape juice and jelly, dill pickles and relish, preserves, peaches, tomatoes, garden beans—their blue cast and Mason tops dimming beneath dust and cobwebs . . . food for a family.

The old house sighed and settled to its outward corners, warmed.

Facing the street and the elms, the twin living and dining rooms were dissected by a stairwell going upward toward the back rooms which we rented to college boarders and to the single upstairs bathroom for which we frequently waited, cracking the door of the unheated bedroom and peering across the hall for signs of vacancy or occupancy.

The living room was dark, papered in green; a baby grand piano filled the small space along with a brown mohair couch, a television set, two overstuffed chairs, a maple end table. There was even a rug on this floor, an old brown and cream threadbare oriental. The dining room at the northeast corner was lighter. A replica Queen Anne's table and chairs and sideboard (garage sale finds) lent a slight elegance to the unmatched rest of the place. And it was here in this house, at this table, in these rooms where my Sunday memories began.

My father was the choir director at First Baptist Church, and we always left home on Sunday morning to the flurry of frantic, last-minute departures. Then came Sunday school, the morning worship, Father leading the singing, the long pews, the anthems, the light diffused through the stained-glass window showing Christ in the Garden of Gethsemane. The hour multiplied by waiting. At last, the final hymn, the altar call, the divesting of choir robes, the storing of sheet music . . . friends, greetings, laughter. Then home to Sunday dinner, to the dining room and the assorted patterns of plates, glassware, serving dishes; Mother, hot, steamy, preoccupied with finishing cooking, her cheeks flushed, the crease line in her forehead deepening; finally the call to dinner, gathering together around the table: brother, sister, friends, relatives, my father at the head; the blessing, the quiet, the passing of fried chicken, mashed potatoes, Jell-O salads, milk gravy, corn bread; and afterwards, a Sunday afternoon nap.

My husband says that all our childhood memories of Sunday tend to be idyllic; however, he remembers the starched shirts against his tender boy's neck, the scratchy woolen pants, the seemingly interminable boredom of Sunday worship. And my own memories are not all dipped in golden glows. For truthfully, Sunday was an exhausting day, and I only knew how exhausting when I became an adult myself and began to wonder how Mother had managed those elaborate dinners on top of a full-time job and busy Saturdays. I particularly learned

how draining a day Sunday could be when David
entered the pastorate and we became responsible for
churches of our own.

We went back into the city of Chicago in 1967 and
started a church where we would be free to experiment
with contemporary forms of worship, to discover means
by which we could relate the gospel to the social issues
which were paramount to our time. After a year and a
half of discussion, twenty-seven of us met one stormy
February day on the west side of the city, in the welcoming premises of the Teamster's Union Hall, Local 705.
Their ballroom became our sanctuary, their barroom our
Christian education facility, the ladies' lounge served as
our nursery. It was not an auspicious beginning.

We were a multiracial congregation with a multiracial
staff. The a capella choir sang from the back of the auditorium; and the soul choir processed to the front wearing
dashikis and moving in rhythm to the piano accompani-
ment of a heavy left-handed bass. These were the years
when the west side of the city went up in smoke during
the riots that followed the assassination of Dr. Martin
Luther King, Jr. Whole crumbling dwellings disappeared in the conflagration and are still empty rubble
today. David's office was burglarized three separate
times. The headquarters of the militant Black Panther
organization was a few blocks away as was Malcolm X
University. We began Circle Church when David was
thirty years of age; the average age of the congregation
was twenty-eight. Within two years, we had grown to
two hundred; at the end of ten years when David resigned, we were a healthy five hundred dreamers.

During these years, people would frequently comment, "Your husband is so intense" or "David is one of
the proverbial angry young men." The verse from
Psalms used to describe Christ when he threw the
money-changers out of the temple was an apt description
for my husband as well, "Zeal for thy house has con-

sumed me" (69:9). He was determined to bring reformation, renewal to the local church, to make it significant
in society and to restore to worship the awed participation of the creature adoring the Creator.

Like so many others before us, we wanted to create a
better place. We questioned everything within the firm
doctrinal boundaries of belief. We sought to work with
the old forms, discard those that had no value, and infuse
those that still made sense with meaning. Being different for the sake of being different was not the purpose
for our creative strivings; but being meaningful was—
meaningful was an all-important word to us as used, for
instance, in *meaningful* worship.

All our worship services were planned around a key
biblical truth and a desired response. The key biblical
truth was the pastor's sermon reduced to a sentence. This
had to be in embryonic form by Wednesday for initial
work at the morning staff meeting, and because post-
cards had already been mailed inviting ten different lay
members of the congregation to gather on Wednesday
evening to brainstorm the Sunday morning sermon and
service. When David was sure that his biblical sermon
thrust was relevant to this lay planning group (the sermon was often altered at this time), then he and the
group would continue to plan the service of worship and
response.

In relation to the key biblical truth, the planning
group would choose a pertinent attribute for which to
praise God, and it would decide what were the most
meaningful ways in which a congregation could do this.
A significant and helpful response would also be designed. Most of our congregation felt that traditional
altar calls had grown counter-productive and so surveys
were created, take-home sheets, self-examination tests,
postcard accountability responses—anything that would
help a congregation integrate the key biblical truth of
that morning into their daily lives. Those planning the

worship services participated themselves Sunday after
Sunday using their unique and individual abilities.
David would take these initial service ideas back to the
staff which would hone them, design the music to fit
the theme, and make all things ready to worship the
Lord with *meaningful* worship.

The result of this weekly activity was an explosion of
the gifts of the congregation in worship Sunday after
Sunday. If you are a professional photographer and no
one has ever invited you to create a worship presenta-
tion, you can imagine the excitement you might feel if
there finally is a place for your ability. We used mime in
our worship services, as well as dance, drama, speech
choirs, artwork, original liturgies, film, antiphonal
Scripture readings, chants, creative prayer forms. Our
music ran the gamut from Bach to rock, from classical
church anthems to selections from the musical *Godspell.*
We used our children—they ushered, they prayed, they
were interviewed, they sang.

Good worship planning was work for us all, staff and
lay people alike. For ten years we had no building of our
own, so crews arrived at seven o'clock each Sunday
morning to clean up the refuse from the dinner dances
held many Saturday nights in the Union Hall. Chairs had
to be set up, the platform dragged to the corner, hymn
books taken from their racks and put in place. If anything visual was needed in terms of media production,
huge black plastic sheeting was draped on the two-story
windows in order to cut out light glare. With little storage space, everything had to be carted, transported,
hauled, lifted, carried, pushed, and shoved into the
meeting hall.

We discovered that people will work at worship and
willingly labor to create an environment for adoration if
they are given half a chance, if they are invited to use
their abilities as gifts unto the Lord, and if the experience becomes significant to them.

One of the deadliest blows to worship is the worshiper as spectator. The biblical ethic regards worship as work. *Av'dh* in Hebrew, *dienst* in German, *leitourgia* in Greek, *service* in English all have the double meaning of worship and work. In fact, *liturgy* means "common work"— a sacred work in which the people cooperate with the divine, a work together which first and foremost brings joy to the Godhead, and second, enormous holy satisfaction to the human workers.

David and I believe that the work of worship can involve all the senses . . . there should be the appeal of the aesthetic to the eyes and the ears; there should be touch; there should be an involvement of the sense of smell; there should be the active collaboration of the intellect where the mind is challenged by the unexpected, by eager mental stimulation with Scripture; there should be physical activity—kneeling, walking to the altar, standing to pray; there should be an emotional commitment with the giving of one's feelings, one's inner passions to active adoration. We had a decade, without any restrictions but self-imposed ones, to invite the body of Circle Church to participate in this "common work of the people."

In short, we were intensely involved in making Sunday special for those ten years that we worked at Circle Church. We were privileged to approach the task from the position of the professional, able to influence the decisions regarding environment, procedures, and the philosophy of Sunday morning worship. But David has always been prophetic in his vision, seeing down the span of time ten to fifteen years ahead of himself. He began to be restless in his pastoral position, and by means of many hard crunches, the Lord eventually led us out of the local church into a national radio ministry.

Suddenly, we were now lay people in terms of Sunday worship. How could the lay person influence the church when the Sunday experience was less than meaningful?

The answer to this began with a farewell gift from the people of Circle Church when we resigned their pastorate. Their gift to us was a trip for two to Israel. Being obnoxious about originality, we determined not to import our Christianity but to turn our once-in-a-lifetime opportunity into a cross-cultural experience. So in the fall of 1977, we joined an El Al tour, the only Gentiles to crash the Jewish tour bus, and one of us a Christian minister at that! Our guide, a *sabra* (Israeli-born), took an extreme nationalistic approach to history and reported a fractured version of even Old Testament events. One of my favorite memories is of David sitting in the back of the bus with a Jewish Rothschild wine dealer and opening his Bible and saying, "Well, actually what really happened was . . . "

On Wednesday we began to hear comments such as, "Oh, Shabbat will be in Tel Aviv. Shabbat will be in Tel Aviv." Sure enough, on Friday afternoon, we checked into a hotel in Tel Aviv and joined some new Orthodox Jewish friends to participate in the evening Sabbath meal. I will never forget the lovely linen cloths on the dining tables, the yarmulkes on the men's heads, the Hebrew blessing over the wine, the prayer over the broken bread, the lighting of the candles.

All my spiritual life I have hunted for the holy, and I have become rather adept at knowing such moments when I find them. This was one. A veil parted and I glimpsed through it, back, back, back into a ritual that had profound and imperative meaning. After celebrating the Jewish Shabbat, I was never to be quite the same again in my understanding of the Christian Sunday observance.

When we returned from our ten-day trip, David began to research the meaning of the Jewish Sabbath. He discovered that Sabbath for the devout Jew (Friday evening at sundown to Saturday evening at sundown) was so special it took three days to anticipate it. (On

Wednesday our tour companions were saying, "Ah,
Shabbat will be in Tel Aviv.") Three days to look forward
to Sabbath, then the high point, the day itself, then for
observant Jews, it was so special, they took three days to
reflect back on its wonder. This three-day anticipation,
then the high point Sabbath, then this three-day reflection created what David has come to term, the rhythm of
the sacred. Illustrated it looks like this:

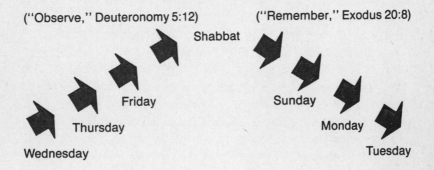

("Observe," Deuteronomy 5:12)   ("Remember," Exodus 20:8)

Shabbat

Friday   Sunday

Thursday   Monday

Wednesday   Tuesday

The rhythm of the sacred with its holy anticipation—
what a contrast to the typical Mains' family Sunday
morning scenario in which the children invariably lost
a dress shoe, or couldn't find their church school lessons; where someone would say the wrong word in the
wrong tone and there would be an angry flare-up, and
we would sit in wooden silence in the car waiting for
the stirred emotions to settle so we could get over being mad in time to worship the Lord in the beauties of
holiness.

I used to think this Sunday morning commotion
("Mo-om! Randy won't let me in the bathroom." BANG!
BANG! "Hurry up! I gotta get in there!") was due to the
fact that we were a ministerial family and some unbid-
den demonic force attempted to steal our good intents
toward adoration. ("Who took my comb?" "Someone
didn't put the milk back in the refrigerator last night!")

I used to think it was all my problem—I was a nice
woman but a bad manager; and my awkwardness in running a household showed most on Sunday morning.
("Mo-om, I can't find any good stockings!" "You know I
hate [those pants, that dress, this shirt, etc.]") I even
identified with Martha in the Scripture story where
Christ comes to visit the home of Lazarus and his two
sisters. ("Mo-om, I don't wanna go to church today. I
think I'm sick.") I knew what it meant to live with a
Mary, except that my Mary was my husband.

I would hustle and bustle, find the missing shoe, iron
the shirt that had been neglected the night before,
throw the wet clothes into the dryer, set the table for ten
for Sunday dinner, prepare a simple meal for guests, go
over the last-minute preparations for our interracial
Christian Education Center plans, then finally get myself dressed after a most inadequate catch-as-catch-can
family breakfast. David would emerge from his study,
holiness sitting on his brow, anointed to present the
Word of the Lord to our congregation, oozing peace and
equanimity. Oh yes, I knew how Martha felt when Mary
sat at the feet of Jesus.

But then I discovered that many Christian families
(not just those of us in pastoral ministry) had the same
struggles. Sunday morning, leaving for church, was often the worst time in their week.

As a couple, David and I vowed to work together to
restore our observance of the Lord's Day, to seek to make
Sunday the best day of the week, the high point, to struggle to establish this rhythm of the sacred in our lives
as individuals and in our lives as a family. We wanted
Sunday to become the joyful focal point of our weekly
lives.

Now it's important to underline the word joyful. We
did not want to slip back into an old legalism, that grim
old joyless observance of the Lord's Day with its killing
can'ts and *don'ts* and *won'ts* and *shall nots*. That attitude

has done as much to create a dread of worship as anything I know. It was against this kind of legalism Christ had to continually speak. In three of the Gospels his words of reminder and rebuke are recorded, "The Sabbath was made for man, not man for the Sabbath." I wanted the kind of celebration in our family hearts that I read about in Isaiah and Deuteronomy:

"If you . . . call the Sabbath a *delight* . . . if you honor it, not going your own ways . . . then you shall take delight in the Lord . . . " (Isaiah 58:13–14). "You shall *rejoice* in your feasts, you and your son and your daughter" (Deuteronomy 16:14).

So David and I moved slowly but determinedly into recapturing Sunday meaningfulness in our new role as lay people. We refused to schedule meetings on Saturday evenings. If we were traveling, we attempted to return home in time for church on Sunday. We curtailed our social activities; we reminded our teens, "Tomorrow is Sunday; be home early tonight," and we began to establish new family traditions to create activities that would encourage Lord's Day appreciation. Not only were we going absolutely counter to the secular culture of society in which the weekend was viewed hedonistically and narcissistically, but we soon discovered that we were going counter to the secularized culture of the church where a full calendar was viewed as sacred.

In September 1985, *The Christian Reader* printed an article by Joe Bayley titled "Ten Truths to Live By" in which the author wrote advice to Christian parents. Admonition number seven reads:

This one may surprise you, but I believe that *my generation's greatest loss—next to the inviolateness of marriage and the family—has been the sanctity of the Lord's Day.* Mary Lou and I started out our home with a rather serious attempt to "keep the Sabbath holy." No work, no group sports for our children, quiet activities, and sometimes visits with Christian friends and their children. But somewhere along the way we changed, and our attitude became much more secular (or pagan) than Christian (in the sense that I now believe the Bible teaches and that our own parents and earlier generations practiced).

For yourself and for any children God may give you, try to recapture the Lord's Day as a day for rest and deeds of mercy, for retreat from the world; try to turn it into the happiest day of the week.

His advice is well-heeded. Our personal journey into the meaningfulness of the Lord's Day has taken over twenty years. But I am glad David and I set out upon this road. Sunday is once again becoming a holy day—not just in concept, or in idea, or in words but in reality, in surprising, tangible actuality. This has been a journey well worth taking, a pilgrimage into discovery. Now we can rejoice in Sunday; it is a delight—it is indeed becoming for us "the happiest day of the week."

2

Jewish
Sabbath
Tradition

"HOW DO WE KEEP OUR BALANCE?" asks Tevye in the musical *Fiddler on the Roof.* "I can tell you that in one word—tradition. Because of our traditions, here in Anatevka, everyone knows who he is and what God expects him to do . . . how to eat, how to sleep, how even to wear clothes. Tradition! Tradition!"

Jewish essayist Achad Haam as quoted in *Toward an American Theology* (Herbert W. Richardson, ed. 1967, p. 130), underlines the vital function of Sabbath tradition in the history of Judaism, stating: "We can affirm without any exaggeration that the Sabbath has preserved the Jews more than the Jews have preserved the Sabbath. If the Sabbath had not restored to them the soul, renewing every week their spiritual life, they would have become so degraded by the depressing experiences of the workdays, that they would have descended to the last step of materialism and of moral and intellectual decadence."

An overlooked phrase tucked away in Leviticus 23:3 hints at the importance of the home in Sabbath celebrations, "The seventh day is a sabbath of solemn rest, a holy convocation; you shall do no work; it is a sabbath to the Lord *in all your dwellings*" (italics mine). Jacob Z. Lauterbach in *Rabbinic Essays* writes ". . . the main center of the Sabbath observance is in the family circle at the home and many of its ceremonies are calculated to strengthen the bonds of love and affection between the members of the family, to emphasize the parental care and duties, and to increase the filial respect and reverence for parents."

As mentioned in the previous chapter Shabbat is the high point of the Jewish week. There is the rhythm of anticipation, participation, and reflection—three days to look forward to, then Shabbat, then three days to look back upon. Some Jewish writers interpret the different wording in the Deuteronomy and Exodus passages to reflect this cycle. Deuteronomy 5:12 says "Observe . . ." and Exodus 20:8 says, "Remember . . ." Both nuances are captured in the sacred rhythm of the Jewish week, not a one-time but a lifetime renewal of a commitment to God.

This rhythm of the sacred made enormous sense to David and myself. After working for years at creating meaningful worship, we still recognized the fact that if people were not prepared to worship, if they had been up late the night before partying or watching Saturday night TV movies, or if their Sunday morning departure was anything like the Mains' (no matter how well-planned the service), it was exceedingly difficult for them to be more than yawning pew-sitters on Sunday morning.

In order to get the most out of the worship experiences, one has to be prepared to worship. Now I realize that many different doors open onto a deeper understanding of Sunday, but for this book I have chosen the door of the Jewish pattern. Perhaps taking a closer look will explain why this tradition stirs David and myself so deeply.

The Jewish pattern is one that demands preparation, both physically and attitudinally. This starts as early as the middle of the week when on Wednesday the prayers and psalms that are recited anticipate the next Shabbat; but it particularly takes on somewhat frantic proportions on Friday, Erev Shabbat (Sabbath Eve), with cleaning, cooking, polishing, washing, setting the table, etc. Luke infers this custom in his account of Joseph of Arimathea taking Christ's body down from the cross: "It was the day of Preparation, and the sabbath was beginning" (Luke 23:54).

During the twenty-four hour cycle of Shabbat itself (from twilight Friday to twilight Saturday) there are three separate plateaus—Friday evening dinner, Saturday morning synagogue worship, and the Saturday afternoon observances—all of which in Orthodox Jewish tradition have rich symbolic customs and overtones.

Most simplistically, Shabbat begins Friday evening when *she* is welcomed to the first meal in the words of the evening service, "and may Israel rest in *her*." Shabbat is welcomed in its feminine aspect, as a bride, a symbolic royal queen. The mood of this first service is infused with the aura of a wedding. This is a family time, it is communal (guests are considered to be a blessing—a *mitzvah*), the physical is ascendant (good food, candlelight, new clothes), the mood is relaxed and joyful, all are making the transition from the material workweek into this special time set apart for the spiritual.

Saturday morning is devoted to the synagogue (if there is a *minyan*, a quorum of ten men). Here reading from the Torah is central to the service. The mood is reflective, listening, quiet, more intellectual. The feminine imagery of the night before gives way to the masculine, in the words of the morning service, "And may

Israel rest in *Him*." There is a meal following this, generally lighter than the Friday meal.

Saturday afternoon/evening is what one writer calls
"Torah-dreamy," meditative. The pulls of the physical
have declined, and the spiritual is on the ascendancy.
Now there is an ability to concentrate on messianic
thoughts, on the Messiah who will redeem the world and
bring universal peace and rest. There is an afternoon
service (prayers and readings), followed by a very simple
meal, then finally, the evening service in which Shabbat
is bid farewell. At the close of the service it is customary
to wish everyone a *shavuah tov* or a *gut vawch* (Hebrew
and Yiddish for "a good week").

To make it a good week, the Jew attempts to sustain
the experience of Shabbat by carrying it into the forth-
coming workweek, holding to the memory of the peace
and set-apartness of the seventh day. In *Tradition and
Contemporary Experience: Essays on Jewish Thought
and Life* edited by Alfred Jospe, Norman E. Firmer
writes, "The Jew bids a plaintive farewell to this great
day, but with zeal replenished and faith renewed. For
his eyes are now lifted to a new Shabbat, a distant yet
beckoning Shabbat, when life will be holy and one, humanity whole and one, and God's Name perfect and one"
(p. 268).

This abbreviated explanation hardly does justice to
the rich inheritance known to those of the Jewish tradition; yet it should serve as a good backdrop for what
David and I learned about making Sunday more meaningful. It was never our purpose to duplicate Jewish tradition. This I want to emphasize. Reformers at heart, we
sought to adapt whatever would make our own participation in Sunday, the Lord's Day, most special. There
were two results we were seeking to achieve:

1. We wanted to make Sunday the high point of the
   week.

2. We wanted to begin our preparations for Sunday morning on Saturday.

While analyzing our own family patterns, David and I felt: one, we needed to establish a tradition for ourselves and the children in order to make a symbolic statement that Sunday was not a day just like any other day of the week; two, we needed to learn about and integrate into our lives the sacred rhythm of anticipation, participation, and reflection; and three, we needed a bridge that would link the Old Testament teaching with the New. We decided that a Sabbathlike Saturday evening meal would help to achieve all three purposes. So with much effort, going against the grain of our already firmly established neglectful habits, with little encouragement from the local church or few positive precedents, and after much trial and error, we established as one of our Sunday preparation concepts a family dinner, held once a month on Saturday evening. We invited my sister and brother-in-law and their two boys to participate with us because we wanted to see if our idea would work, not only in our nuclear family with older children, but in a situation that would include younger grade-schoolers.

Before explaining the lovely Saturday evening tradition that is evolving in our family, however, it will first be helpful to establish an overview of customary Jewish practices; and since specific suggestions vary according to the source, I have synthesized the following agenda as a general summary.

A JEWISH SABBATH OVERVIEW

1. First, there is the lighting of the candles which is traditionally done by the wife, mother, or woman of the house. There are two candles symbolizing the words, *observe* and *remember*. These are usually lit in the time

frame from one and a quarter hours to eighteen minutes before sunset. A prayer she might pray before lighting the candles is:

> O God of Your people Israel: You are holy
> And You have made the Shabbat and the people of
>   Israel holy.
> You have called upon us to honor the Shabbat with
>   light,
> With joy, and with peace—
> As a king and queen give love to one another;
> As a bride and her bridegroom—
> So we have kindled these two lights for love of your
> daughter, the Shabbat day.
> Almighty God,
> Grant me and all my loved ones
> A chance to truly rest on this Shabbat day.
> May the light of the candles drive out from among us
> The spirit of anger, the spirit of harm,
> Send your blessings to my children,
> That they may walk in the ways of Your Torah, Your
>   light.
> May You ever be their God, and mine, O Lord.
> My Creator and my Redeemer. Amen
>
>> Translated from the Yiddish by Arthur Green
>> Reprinted from *The Jewish Catalog*

After the candles are lit, she says "Blessed are You, Lord our God, King of the Universe, who has sanctified us with His commandments, and commanded us to light the Shabbat candles." With minor changes, this lovely beginning for the evening is extremely adaptable to a Christian tradition.

2. The Kabalat Shabbat is an ancient prayer service made of introductory psalms and the psalm for the Sabbath day. The evening service follows including the central reference to the creation theme and when this is concluded it is customary to wish one another *gut*

shabbos or *shabbat shalom*—"a good Shabbat" or "peaceful Shabbat."

3. The blessing of the children is one of the traditions that specifically strengthen familial bonds. A Jewish child whose parents keep this tradition know that if he is not affirmed or touched by his father the rest of the week, on this one night at least, he will experience the words and embrace of love. The father places his lips on the child's forehead and holds him while saying, "May God make you like Ephraim and Menassah" (for males) and "May God make you like Sarah, Rebekah, Rachel, and Leah" (for females).

4. At this point the family sings "Peace Be unto You"—a welcome to the angels who accompany the meeting of humans and the bride, Shabbat.

5. The husband blesses his wife using the words from the verses of Proverbs 31:10–31.

6. The wine is blessed using the Kiddush—a prayer of sanctification for the Sabbath.

7. There is a ritual hand washing and then the blessing over the challot, the traditional braided bread.

8. The meal is eaten and *enjoyed* with singing and much laughter.

9. A grace is said when the meal is ended, an official closure based on Deuteronomy 8:10, "When you have eaten your fill, give thanks to the Lord your God for the good land which He has given you."

10. The rest of the evening before bedtime is usually spent talking to family and friends and/or in the study of the Torah.

Many of these customs related to the Friday Shabbat meal find satisfactory Christian fulfillment. The lighting of the candles can represent Christ's light as it came into our darkened world; the broken bread and the blessing over the bread can recall scriptures in which Christ declared he was the bread of life; the wine (or a substitute juice for those who abstain from alcohol) can sym-

bolize the fact that Christ declared he was the vine and
his father the vinedresser. A Christian evening service
on Saturday can be designed around a meal that will
keep the spirit of Sabbath but prepare us for Sunday by
pointing to the One who is the culmination of all our
spiritual memorials. Prayers can be written and scriptures read that will turn our hearts toward Sunday and,
at the same time, amplify for ourselves, our friends, and
our children the true meaning of observing the Lord's
Day with Sabbath remembrance.

David and I love to create new forms for old spiritual
truths. We have adapted many ideas from the traditional
Jewish Friday Shabbat meal to a Saturday evening meal
that turns our hearts and minds toward Sunday. Our
results will be included in the next chapter as a framework for creativity. Many people love the energizing
that comes from the struggle to create new approaches;
others, I realize, prefer to work with an already established format. Some are even threatened by the change
that accompanies creative restructuring. The following
Order of Worship is for those people who (for whatever
reason) prefer not to develop their own format.

An Order of Worship
for the Evening before the Lord's Day

(Candlesticks on the table include at least two candles.
A goblet of wine—or juice—is placed near the candlestick. Two loaves of bread, homebaked if possible, wait
beneath a white cloth.)

(*All stand.*)
Host: Light and peace in Jesus Christ our Lord.
All: Thanks be to God
Host: If I say, "Surely the darkness will cover me, and
the light around me turn to night," darkness is not dark
to you, O Lord; the night is as bright as the day; dark-

ness and light to you are both alike. (See Psalm 139:
10–11.)

(Remain standing.)
Prayer for Light

Host: Let us pray.
All: O Lord God Almighty, as you have taught us to call
the evening, the morning, and the noonday one day; and
have made the sun to know its going down; dispel the
darkness of our hearts, that by your brightness we may
know you to be the true God and eternal light, living and
reigning forever and ever.
Amen.

(Be seated.)
The lighting of the Lord's Day Lights

(Blessings by the hostess before lighting the candles.)
Creation Candle
This candle represents creation.
Blessed art You, O Lord our God,
King of the Universe,
who brings forth light out of darkness.

Redemption Candle
This candle represents redemption.
Jesus said: "I am the light of the world."
Our Lord said, "You are the light of the world."
As we light these candles and set them to give light to
all who are in this house, light our lives with the great
love of your Son, Jesus, in whose name we pray. Amen.

(The wife lights the candles.)

(The father makes a compliment to his wife and all wives
present.)

An excellent wife, who can find? For her worth is far
above jewels. . . . She looks well to the ways of her
household, and does not eat the bread of idleness. Her
children rise up and bless her; her husband also, and he

praises her saying: "Many daughters have done nobly, but you excel them all." . . . A woman who fears the Lord, she shall be praised (Proverbs 31:10, 27–30 NASB).

(The father recites the prayer over the drink.)

Blessed are You, O Lord our God, King of the Universe, who creates the fruit of the vine.

(All drink as a common cup is passed.)

(Beginning with the father, each person in turn repeats the blessing over the bread.)

Blessed are You, O Lord our God, King of the Universe who brings forth bread from the earth.

(The bread is passed, then the meal is shared with joy, laughter, and conversation.)

(Said by all standing.)
Grace after the meal

Blessed are You, O Lord our God, King of the Universe, who provides the fruit of the earth for our use.
We bless you for fulfilling continually your promise that while the earth remains, seedtime and harvest shall not fail.

Teach us to remember that it is not by bread alone that we live. Grant us evermore to feed on Him who is the true bread from heaven, even Jesus Christ our Lord. Amen.

Celebrate the Feasts by Martha Zimmerman gives Christian celebrations for Old Testament festivals. The author includes a detailed explanation of Jewish Sabbath customs with menus and recipes for meals. She also outlines a Saturday evening ritual which suggests a song to be sung after the father's compliment to his wife.

Jewish writers say that the world is resouled every
Shabbat, in other words, the spiritual emphasis begins to
ascend, and the material pulls, weekday thoughts, responsibilities, habits, work mentality, job worries, begin
to withdraw. Abraham J. Heschel writes, "Every seventh
day a miracle comes to pass, the resurrection of the soul,
of the soul of man and of the soul of all things" (*The
Sabbath: Its Meaning for Modern Man* 1966, p. 83).
Rabbi Samuel H. Dresner says the Sabbath is "one of the
surest means of finding peace in the war-torn realm
of the soul . . . an idea with infinite potentiality, infinite power, infinite hope. . . . Through the Sabbath,
Judaism has succeeded in turning its greatest teachings
into a day. Out of a remote world of profound thoughts,
grand dreams and fond hopes—all of which seem so distant, so intangible and so unrealizeable—the Sabbath
has forged a living reality which can be seen and tasted
and felt once a week."

The spiritualizing aspect of Sabbath observance is
poignantly recalled by Issac Grunfeld in *The Sabbath: A
Guide to Its Understanding and Observance:* "The train
dragged on with human freight. Pressed together like
cattle in the crowded trucks, the unfortunate occupants
were unable even to move. The atmosphere was stifling.
As the Friday afternoon wore on, the Jews and Jewesses
in the Nazi transport sank deeper and deeper into their
misery. Suddenly an old Jewish woman managed with a
great effort to move and open a bundle. Laboriously she
drew out—two candlesticks and two challot. She had
just prepared them for the Sabbath when she was
dragged from her home that morning. They were the
only things she had thought worthwhile taking with her.
Soon the Sabbath candles lit up the faces of the tortured
Jews and the song of 'Lekhah Dodi' transformed the
scene. Sabbath with its atmosphere of peace had descended upon them all."

I have known that Sabbath peace myself, that "re-souling of the world." It descends almost tangibly each time I withdraw from the chaffing hustle and bustle of human existence, each time I purposely prepare myself for Sunday, when I go to the effort of anticipation, participation, and reflection. Each time I reach out this peace touches me.

About now I can just hear someone protesting, "But Christians have a Sunday tradition, the Lord's Day. We go to church. Most of us are faithful attenders." That is true, but that tradition is in grave danger of losing its meaning. We are becoming like the Israelites against whom the prophets cried, "You call this a fast, and a day acceptable to the Lord? . . . If you turn back your foot from the sabbath, from doing your pleasure on my holy day, and call the sabbath a delight and the holy day of the Lord honorable; if you honor it, not going your own ways, or seeking your own pleasure, or talking idly; then you shall take delight in the Lord" (Isaiah 58:5, 13, 14).

The truth is: There are fewer and fewer Christians who call the Lord's Day a delight, who no longer use the day for their own pleasure, who keep the holy day of the Lord honorable, who do not go their own ways, seek their own pleasure, talk idly. In a Chapel of the Air interview, British Revivalist Leonard Ravenhill told David the story of staff prayer before the Sunday morning service in a large Texas church in which he was speaking. As the ministers were waiting to step onto the platform, one of them asked the others, "Well do you think the Cowboys are going to win this afternoon?" The way you react to this comment is a good test of whether or not you really regard Sunday as a holy day; holy men, doing holy work on a holy day should be concentrating on holy thoughts. They should be asking, "How do we worship ourselves at this time in such a way that we lead these people into adoration?"

Unfortunately, it seems that everything else but Sunday is the high point of our week: time in the garden, a shopping trip, concerts, vacation homes, high school sports, dinner out with friends, the doubles' tennis challenge, finishing the latest project, Sunday afternoon football on TV, jobs. We rarely begin to anticipate Sunday as early as Thursday, thinking with delight, *Ah, Sunday is coming! Sunday will be . . . Sunday will be!* Rarely do we ask ourselves, *What can we do to make this coming Sunday the best day of this week?*

Through the years of pogroms and dispersions, of persecutions and betrayal, it is not the Jewish family that has kept the Sabbath, but the Sabbath which has kept the Jewish family—a concept in these increasingly secularized days that it would do well for those of us of Christian heritage to seriously consider.

3

Lord's Day Eve

"SATURDAY MORNING WAS COME, and all the summer world was bright and fresh and brimming with life. There was a song in every heart; and if the heart was young, the music issued at the lips." So begins Mark Twain's chapter on the classic tale of Tom Sawyer whitewashing Aunt Polly's fence. When Tom surveyed the thirty-yard fence he was to whitewash "all gladness left him, and a deep melancholy settled down upon his spirit."

However, after attempting to bribe his pal Jim to do his task, (the intent of which is interrupted by Aunt Polly and her flailing slipper), Tom has a great, magnificent inspiration. Ben Rogers looms into sight, on his way to go swimming, leering, "Hello, old chap, you got to work, hey?"

Tom replies, "What do you call work? . . . Does a boy get to whitewash a fence every day?" He sweeps his brush daintily back and forth, surveying the effect, adding a dab here and there, until Ben finally offers his half-eaten apple as an incentive to turn over the brush; which Tom does reluctantly while murmuring, "Aunt Polly's awful particular about this fence—right here on the street, you know—but if it was the back fence I wouldn't mind, and she wouldn't . . . I reckon there ain't one boy in a thousand, maybe two thousand, that can do it the way it's got to be done."

By the end of the afternoon, Tom's magnificent idea has rewarded him with twenty different items, among them "a kite in good repair, a dead rat, and a string to swing it with, twelve marbles, . . . a key that wouldn't unlock anything, a fragment of chalk, a glass stopper of a decanter, a tin soldier, a couple of tadpoles. . . . "

Twain concludes by commenting, "He had had a nice, good, idle time all the while—plenty of company—and the fence had three coats of whitewash on it! If he hadn't run out of whitewash, he would have bankrupted every boy in the village."

When it comes to teaching children spiritual truth, I am definitely of the Tom Sawyer school. I think it is a sin to make spiritual things boring! I believe the Scriptures mean what they say when they use the phrases, "You shall *delight* in your feasts, you and your sons and daughters" or "if you call the sabbath a *delight*" (italics mine). It is not enough to create a spiritual activity; I want the children to enjoy it. An old axiom goes: What's learned with pleasure is learned full measure. If it looks enjoyable, people want to be a part of it, and they learn in the process.

Too often, Sundays have been made dreadful because of legalistic inhibitions; the gorgeous spirit of celebration has been squeezed dry. The word *solemn* as it is used in Leviticus 23:3, "but on the seventh day is a sabbath of solemn rest" has been interpreted by legalists to mean dour-faced, pucker-mouthed, *tut-tut* negations. I believe the word means that we are to take the Sabbath commandments seriously, not that we are to go around acting serious, hermetically sealed off from Sunday joy.

This severe approach always makes us abhor the very thing we are supposed to love. Long ago, it angered Christ.

When David and I first began our Saturday evening preparations as early measures in our personal approach to renewing Sunday meaning, we wanted it to be a celebration of spiritual life. Our four children ranged in ages from older grade schoolers to young adults in college. My sister and her husband (co-workers with us in our radio ministry) and their two younger boys joined us to begin carving out a family Sabbathlike experience. During our first trial run, one of their little boys kept whispering, "When can we go home?" and the other plunked on the piano—a sure sign that we needed a Tom-Sawyer-like idea to help them enjoy these family ventures.

We have designed our Lord's Day Eve times to appeal to the youngest child. Adult tolerance for child-oriented activities is much greater than child tolerance for adult-oriented activities. At any rate, since we made this modification to adapt our agenda to the participation of the youngest child, my sister's two boys eagerly look forward to the Lord's Day Eve meals at Uncle David and Aunt Karen's. (And I haven't heard older offspring complaining, either—the "fence painting" is going well.)

David and I are good at creative approaches; most of the spiritual training of our children has been the organic kind, a fit teaching or application or discussion at the point of the child's experience. However, we have never been successful in terms of establishing what has traditionally been termed the "family altar" if what is meant by that is a set time in which a paterfamilias draws his spouse and children near and reads Scripture and prays. Please understand, I have nothing against this approach as long as it does not develop spiritual resistance in the offspring. Some families employ family devotional times very well; it was just not a style that fit our renegade tribe. We have been much better at spiritual spontaneity, at designing activities that get the fence whitewashed, that develop disciplines without their seeming to be work.

However, I am beginning to appreciate established forms. There is comfort in not having to originate new ideas all the time, to have an established family liturgy, a framework within which to work. Jewish writers say that Shabbat has both *Malkah* (the law) and *Kallah* (inner love). The *Malkah*, the form, insures success; a person's inward mood is easily subject to change—the *Malkah* provides stability, to guarantee the mood, to lend permanence to Shabbat feelings. "On the other hand," writes Rabbi Samuel H. Dresner, "the law of Malkah, without the love of the Kallah would mean a harsh, officious, legalistic day . . . 'Remember the Sabbath day'—in your heart and soul with joy and love and inner peace; 'Observe the Sabbath day'—keep its laws and statutes with devotion and loyalty and steadfastness" (*The Sabbath* [Burning Bush Press, 1970], p. 26).

Consequently, we have designed a framework for our Lord's Day Eve meal within which there is latitude for creativity. David and my brother-in-law, Steve, divide the responsibilities, then make assignments to all who are going to be present (even with careful planning, absenteeism is not always avoidable—adolescent activities and our travel schedules are both powerful sources of competition); but nevertheless, determination has its own rewards, and our monthly meal has become a family tradition which is meaningful to all, the responsibility for which is shared by all participants.

The meal itself varies depending on the economics available, the energy-drain of the last week and just how much is going on that Saturday. We want to avoid the temptation of attempting to create a Christmas-like celebration once a month. My sister, Valerie, and I may share the meal responsibilities; if she's too busy, I may make a pot of chili or if I'm too busy, she may create a simple casserole. We bake potatoes and provide toppings, organize make-your-own-sandwich menus. We have even observed this extended family tradition in restaurants when the work load of the week has been too heavy for the planning and preparation of a special dinner.

This is not to say we haven't also had lovely evenings with flower centerpieces, linens and silver, crystal and china plates, and the more-than-extra gourmet effort. But the point is: it is not so important what we eat as that we eat together.

The agenda for this celebration goes like this with the responsibility for planning each of these items shared by the adults and the children:

1. The lighting of the candles.
2. The blessing over the meal.
3. The meal with specially planned table conversation.
4. The blessing of the children (and sometimes spouses).
5. The God Hunt for children.
6. The God Hunt for adults (with younger children excused to play with toys in the Sabbath basket).
7. A prayer in preparation for Sunday.

The idea, of course, behind all this forming of new tradition is that we are preparing ourselves to meet with Christ in a special way the next day when the church is gathered.

THE LIGHTING OF THE CANDLES

The lighting of the candles symbolizes that our evening has begun, and that the light of Christ's pres-

ence is now among us in a special way. The youngest
children take turns lighting the candles and, at the
evening's end, extinguishing them. I bought a brass five-
branched candlestick especially for our Saturday meals
so that the candle-lighter would feel his job was special.

Someone has been given the assignment to choose a
scripture or some other selection to read while this goes
on. I am always on the lookout for poems, appropriate
quotes and verses. Many scriptures deal with Christ being the light of the world. *The Book of Common Prayer*
has been a rich resource. The offices of "Daily Evening
Prayer" and "Compline" include appropriate prayers
and collects. For example:

O Gracious Light *Phos hilaron*

O gracious Light,
pure brightness of the everliving Father in heaven,
O Jesus Christ, holy and blessed!

Now as we come to the setting of the sun,
and our eyes behold the vesper light,
we sing thy praises, O God: Father, Son, and Holy Spirit.

You are worthy at all times to be praised by happy voices,
O Son of God, O Giver of life,
and to be glorified through all the worlds.

A Collect for Saturdays
O God, the source of eternal light: Shed forth your un-
ending day upon us who watch for you, that our lips may
praise you, our lives may bless you, and our worship on
the morrow give you glory; through Jesus Christ our
Lord. Amen.

An Evening Prayer
Almighty God, we give you thanks for surrounding us,
as daylight fades, with the brightness of the vesper

light; and we implore you of your great mercy that, as
you enfold us with the radiance of this light, so you
would shine into our hearts the brightness of your Holy
Spirit; through Jesus Christ our Lord. Amen.

THE BLESSING OVER THE MEAL

The blessing over the meal can be a spoken prayer, or
it can be sung. Again this is decided by whoever is assigned this section of responsibility. This is a time when
children can easily participate. We have often given a
word of thanksgiving for the person seated to our right
or prayed sentence prayers around the table with a given
starter phrase: "This is what I like about you, Christ
. . ." and requested that each one fill in the phrase on
his or her own.

TABLE CONVERSATION

Since dinner table conversation in families has a tendency to bounce and ricochet, we try to make sure that a
portion of our discussion is guided. Long ago, when the
children were small, we made a rule that at the table
there would only be one subject discussed at a time;
when we were finished with that topic then we would
move on to the next. This prevented the two-or-three-
ring circus effect, with main events and sideshows going
on at once; the rule insured that all who cared to speak
could and that anyone who spoke would be heard by all.

Some of the assignments at our Lord's Day Eve meal
have included choosing an adjective to describe the person on our right, then telling why we chose that word.
Another time one of the children wrote questions out on
slips of paper and put them into a paper sack; each one
at the table drew a question from the sack and answered.
Some of the questions were:

1. Who is your favorite Bible character and why?
2. If Jesus sat next to you in church tomorrow and you could tell him one thing—what would it be?
3. Do you think that Jesus really did welcome the children or is that just a story?
4. Tell Jesus which you like best—Christmas or Easter —and why.
5. What's one very good lesson Jesus taught you?
6. Who was one of Jesus' best friends?

We've discussed social issues such as abortion and terrorism and their relationship to our faith. At one of our recent Lord's Day Eve meals, David gave us each a sheet of questions to fill out about a different family member; then during table conversation we read what we had written. Here are the kinds of questions we answered:

1. What good thing about this person might he or she not be aware of?
2. How might this person someday benefit the Kingdom?
3. What verse comes to mind when you think of this person?
4. What special individual do you hope this person could someday meet?
5. What experience do you covet for this person?
6. What do you think Jesus might say to this person?

The varieties of table discussion are infinite, but the purpose of this time is to have meaningful table talk in which all can participate. Doloras Curran, in her book *Traits of a Healthy Family*, underscores the fact that one sign of family well-being is good communication patterns, that the "healthy family values table time and conversation". She quotes author George Armelagos bemoaning the modern death of the family table, "Dinner was one of the major times that the parents included children in family and societal affairs. Dinner began with prayer, which put the food in a symbolic and ritualistic context. Then, in the process of talking, social relationships, attitudes and beliefs were all enforced." One family counselor once commented, "The best way to discover the health of a family is to eat a few meals with them. They can't fake it. Too many ingrained eating patterns. Some are miserable, but others are beautiful to behold."

Developing a healthy atmosphere at our dinner table is important to us, and we attempt to have a spiritual tone at this special meal because we want the children to grow up feeling familiar and comfortable with theological language.

THE BLESSING OF THE CHILDREN

The blessing for the children is a profound activity which deserves some explanation. Generally, the fathers design and give the blessing, but at times mothers have given the blessing and even siblings have created words of blessing for one another. These can be special verses from Scripture; they might be a compliment in an area of improvement—"This is where I have seen you have grown, and I want to affirm your growth." Once I told each child the meaning of his/her name and the promise inherent in its choice. We might say at the beginning of a school year, "This is one good thing I want for you this year."

In the book titled *The Blessing*, authors Gary Smalley and John Trent examine Old Testament patriarchal blessings, such as the ones Abraham gave to Isaac and Isaac gave to Jacob and Jacob gave to his sons. Genesis 49 records the emotional moment when the children of

Israel gather by their father's deathbed. Closely examin-
ing such scriptural examples, the authors come to the
conclusion that there are five ingredients common to
patriarchal blessings: (1) There is meaningful touch; (2)
there is a spoken word; (3) there is expressing high
value; (4) there is picturing a special future; and (5)
there is an active commitment on the part of the blesser.

The whole book is built around the proposition that
every child needs to receive his parents' blessing and
that children become faith-crippled when parents with-
hold this blessing. There are some people who go
through life seeking the blessing, who have never had it.
These are those who, all their lives, cry out like Esau,
"Bless me, even me, oh my Father."

Perhaps this explains why this is such a powerful moment in our family Lord's Day Eve meals. Guests in our
home regularly become teary-eyed, often moved beyond
explanation when these words of affirmation and love
are spoken by a parent to a child. No matter how you
design a Sabbathlike family observance, I would make
sure that this one element is always included.

THE GOD HUNT

The God Hunt is the means by which we develop the
capacity in ourselves and in our children to recognize
God's work in our everyday lives. The pattern we have
devised for older people is still too advanced for younger
children (although we are often surprised by their spiritual acuity), so we have adapted activities more fitting
for their ages. Two cards, one for each nephew, are hidden around the living room. The boys scramble to hunt
for God's message for them—a card on which is written
a Scripture verse. When both cards have been finally
found (accompanied by helpful hints, "You're cold;
you're lukewarm. You're hot!"), an object lesson demon-

strates their meaning. For instance, we've wrapped thread around little boys' wrists to show the power of habitual sin. One round of thread can be easily broken, five rounds is harder, fifteen is impossible.

We might read a short story at this time, or act out a verse. We've even hidden pennies to amplify the meaning of Christ's parables on the Kingdom of God being like a precious thing hidden in everyday life circumstances. This part of the evening is specifically designed to relate to the youngest child, and when this is over, the boys are dismissed to play with the toys in what we call the Sabbath basket.

The Sabbath basket is filled with small playthings but can only be used at these special family gatherings, not at other times when the boys are in our home. One of the regular assignments given to the older participants is to add items to the basket (small, inexpensive books, cars, toys) so that there is new pleasure each time it is opened.

Once the boys are dismissed, the older half of the family unit begin to share their God Hunt sightings, and this opens up a whole other level of spiritual communication.

The God Hunt is any time God intervenes in our everyday lives and we recognize it to be Him. Jeremiah 29:13, 14 invites us to this search, "You will seek me and find me; when you seek me with all your heart, I will be found by you. . . ." There are four general categories that help us to sight God's work in our lives. They are:

1. Any obvious answer to prayer.
2. Any unexpected evidence of God's care.
3. Any unusual linkage or timing.
4. Any help to do God's work in the world.

As the family shares ways they have seen God work in their lives in the last weeks, we write this information

down in a journal which we add to each time we gather
for the Lord's Day Eve. What we are giving to ourselves
and to one another by participating in this spiritual activity is the ability to recognize God's daily work in our
everyday lives, what David calls "the naturalness of the
supernatural," as well as a growing comfort in talking
about spiritual matters.

I can't express the power that exists in children hearing their father, mother, uncle, older cousin share these
spiritual sightings. "I have a sighting," someone will say.
"God really answered one of my prayers." Of course, we
don't insist that everyone talk; we all have bad weeks, or
bad days, but there are enough of us that when one
begins, it often triggers remembrance of a recent God
Hunt item in others.

David and I practice the God Hunt every day of our
lives. We write down spiritual sightings in our individual prayer journals; we actively look for his hand to
work in the commonplace experiences of our living. But
we also want the children to know his immediacy, his
ability to personalize his loving care. This time in our
Lord's Day Eve is a moment that fills our hearts with
testimony, amazes us with stories of God's active inter-
vention, and binds us closer together as more than just a
human family, but a family that is part of God's household of faith.

A PRAYER FOR SUNDAY

We attempt to end early, at least by nine o'clock. Our
prayer at the end of the evening is one of thanks for
God's presence in our lives, but also one of intercession.
We pray for the church that will gather across our land
the next day, we pray for our pastors who will be preaching the Word, we pray that our hearts will be prepared
to receive the Word but also be prepared to give worship

and adoration. We end our evening by reminding ourselves to be ready for tomorrow.

This is not just a family event, although it is best observed in community. Singles could begin wonderful bonding traditions by building a similar evening together; Christians living in retirement communities, separated from their children could observe Lord's Day Eve meals together eliminating the loneliness and feelings of alienation that often occur with aging. The potentials for faith-building, for rich spiritual experience and growth are manifold and do not have to be focused only in the nuclear family. Who knows, if you attempt to form your own Sabbathlike celebration, you too may step into a holy moment.

I remember when after years of planning, discussion, testing, and many stops-and-starts, David and I finally pulled our first Lord's Day Eve meal together. I actually was prepared! No last-minute frantic panics, no rushing to the store for a forgotten ingredient. There were actually forty-five minutes to spare before company was due to arrive. I stood in my kitchen and looked out across the dining room with its tables set with lovely fresh cloths, the good Bavarian china inherited from my mother, the goblets, the flower centerpieces, the candles ready for lighting, the pleasant odor of dinner warming in the ovens, the gentle classical music soothing the atmosphere.

My thoughts went back to Tel Aviv and our Jewish friends, to that Shabbat meal several years before which had been so special that it catapulted David and myself into intensive research, thinking, and study. *We are finally going to pull this off,* I thought to myself. *I don't believe it! Shabbat will be . . . Shabbat will be. . . .*

It was then I recognized with my heart the unseen presence. I was not alone in that kitchen. I was startled with spiritual awareness, awed by this hidden reality. And I heard that inward voice that speaks without words, but communes to our deep selves, *You have sought to honor me with your efforts; now I will honor you with my presence.* My eyes began to fill with tears; I swallowed hard against the catch in my throat.

The Jews say that Messiah will not come on Shabbat because he is already present. I suddenly knew why that moment in Tel Aviv had been so holy; why my kitchen and home, these common places, were suddenly alive with the unseen. The Messiah was near. Christ is the Lord of the Sabbath; he truly makes himself known to us when we seek to honor him with our lives.

The Lord of the Sabbath, my Christ, this One I love, will be present in our lives, undefinably but significantly, when we struggle to prepare ourselves to get ready for his coming.

4

Lord's Day
Preparations

I CLEARLY REMEMBER the first time David left without my company to speak in a church for a weekend of meetings. Although I had been David's regular traveling companion, our first infant put an end to my journeyings and was now sound asleep in his crib. I accompanied David down the stairs of our apartment, around the corner of the building, and waved him to the parking lot. Despite myself, tears blurred my sight, and not wanting to send David away with memories of a weeping wife, I tried to smile through them. It was hard to be separated from my young husband.

Although David and I are a strong and compatible team, our marriage has also been keynoted by the separation of distance as one or the other of us has traveled in ministry. A spiritual mentor shared with me that she and her husband were parted six months of the first year of their married life while he opened up the interior of

New Guinea for missionary work. I noted her words then, and I remind myself of them frequently now, "We counted it as joy for the sake of the gospel of Christ."

Because David and I love each other deeply, our homecomings to one another after our constant and frequent travel separations are wonderful. When I return, I return to children and familiarity, but most of all to David; and when he comes home, he comes home to me.

During those early years of travel separations, I counted the moments until David returned. He used to brag to his friends that no matter how late he came home, I was always waiting up for him. Actually, what really happened was that I would go to sleep with the lights on while I waited (young-mother fatigue was a very real factor). But even in deep sleep I sensed when my husband was approaching, and this subjective emotional anticipation triggered an alarm in me that invariably woke me not long before David pulled his car into the driveway. I can't explain this except that it was some early marriage phenomenon—I literally could sense David returning from miles and miles away. I was suddenly awake!—minutes before his car turned into our driveway, before his key was in the lock, before he walked up the stairs to our second-floor apartment. My wakefulness notified me that my beloved was coming home.

Now, after decades of marriage, I don't allow myself to miss David when we are separated—that regular pain of separation would be unbearable for both him and for myself. I don't wake with a start before he returns; he's often in the bedroom before I'm even aware that he has come home. Yet because of the closeness of our relationship there is a sense in which no matter how far we travel from each other, I am not really gone from him, nor is he really gone from me. The emotional, psychological, and spiritual intimacy of our relationship still exists even when we are physically separated. Without communication, I often know when he has needs for urgent prayer and when he's unusually fatigued. And with distance between us, I often have time to *feel* the deep love in my heart for him, whereas when we're near each other, life and schedules and circumstances and people in crises and children interfere.

I am learning to regard our separations "with joy for the sake of the gospel of Christ." We go away from each other, we return in eagerness; we spend cherished time with each other, and this nurtures us for the next parting.

The human cycle of departure and reunion is very much like our experience of the presence of Christ in the Jewish pattern of the rhythm of the sacred. The divine and the human move close to one another when time is set aside for spiritual loving on Sabbath; but there is a distancing that occurs when schedules and work and responsibilities intervene. We, the human, know that God, the divine, is near; he is very much present in our consciousness because of the times we have spent together, but we move closest together when we give one another time. Charted, the rhythm of the week might look something like this:

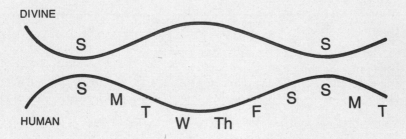

For the last fifteen years, I have conscientiously practiced the presence of Christ. Through the aid of the Holy Spirit, whose ministry on earth is to reveal the reality of Jesus to us, I have attempted to identify Christ in all his

disguises—to see him in the hungry, the thirsty, the es-
tranged, the naked, the sick, or the imprisoned. I've
trained my mind to make the first thoughts of each day
be prayer thoughts before I even rise from the bed; I have
conducted prolonged studies through the Scriptures,
taken time to meditate on his life as revealed in the
Gospels, and searched through the Old Testament for
the messianic promises which point to his coming. Because of this deliberate discipline, I can say that one of
the greatest realities in my life is the life of Christ in the
present tense, Jesus in the here of my life, in the now of
my days.

I have learned that we feel distanced from him when
we don't spend time with him.

I have learned that the more we practice his presence,
the more we experience of his presence.

Let me illustrate this in another way. While preparing
a company dinner last week—putting my plain cream,
wedding Lenox on the aqua place mats; tucking napkins
into the brass rings; experimenting with a new stew
recipe, while persuading one teen to mix the ingredients for homemade gingerbread and the other teen to
peel carrots—I thought, "I feel ready! I feel ready for
company!"

There was even time for a short nap in the afternoon
before our company dinner; for a few moments to sit and
enjoy the fire in the fireplace while I quietly sipped a
glass of spiced cranberry juice.

I feel ready, I thought with deep pleasure. *Ready for
these people who are coming to my home tonight. I feel
prepared, the food is almost done, the table setting is
complete, the candles are waiting to be lit, and favorite
music is playing on the stereo.*

A little reality was injected into this self-satisfied eu-
phoria later in the evening by my eldest son who reminded me during the dinner conversation of times when
I had not been so ready. Randall and I, unfortunately,

grew up together. I turned twenty in the hospital a few days after his birth.

"Mom," he said. "I can remember when you used to get so up-tight with us kids that you'd threaten to leave!"

There was a moment's pause while I considered how I could gracefully counter this accusation. This untimely reminder was spoken in front of our guests, family friends, who (though they have loved our children) have never had children of their own. (You have to live with four kids to know exactly how rugged raising four kids can sometimes be.)

I was grateful that Randall didn't also remind me of all the times I hadn't felt ready for company, of the frantic hour before dinner guests arrived, of the many times I hollered at my family to "get in the kitchen and give me a hand!" I'm sure there was many a conversational memory that could have been plumbed from those unready moments—which were rather frequent because while we were in the pastorate, "company's coming" was standard daily stuff.

And in thinking back on the contrast between the before (not being ready for special guests) and the after (being ready and feeling ready for company), I have wondered what made the difference.

The answer was and is: practice. Lots and lots of practice at getting ready for people who are coming to my house. Practice in the physical mechanics of hospitality— the food and the table. Practice in the spiritual understanding of hospitality—Bible study and thinking about and writing a book on the topic, then teaching seminars across the country and being forced to live out scriptural hospitality or consider myself a hypocrite. Practice in the inner attitude of hospitality—attempting to welcome each person into my life and my home as Christ would welcome them, even to welcome some as though they were Christ.

The practice of hospitality is what has made me so ready to receive special guests.

Practice is also what makes us proficient at recognizing Christ's presence, and this practice takes a lifetime of work. Getting ready to receive the Lord on Sunday in a way that is more special than the other days of the week is one of the means by which we learn to practice his presence. Getting ready for Sunday is a discipline in getting ready for the Lord.

John the Baptist shattered the wilderness of Judea with a loud shout. It was an ancient prophetic cry that had sounded repetitively from the mouths of God's faithful servants. "Get ready! Get ready for the coming of the Lord!" For centuries holy men and women had stood in the wilderness of their own time and culture and shouted in one way or another so that others could hear, "Get ready! The day of the Lord is at hand!"

And that day came, and that Lord stood in synagogues Sabbath after Sabbath; and he absolutely wrenched the pharisaical pet-legalities, the cherished bondages, the spiritualized profanities away from the accumulated accretions of centuries of Sabbath observance. He healed on the Sabbath, invoking the wrath of the demagogues. "And Jesus said to them, 'I ask you, is it lawful on the sabbath to do good or to do harm, to save life or to destroy it?'" (Luke 6:9). Christ knew his father had intended it for a mercy day.

Walking through a grainfield, absorbed in conversation, his disciples casually plucked and ate a few grains of wheat, rubbing them in their hands. This invoked pietistic *uh-uh-uhhuhs*. Christ challenged the proud accumulations of outwardly measured prudity—the endless restrictions of activity on this rest day. "The sabbath was made for man, not man for the sabbath" (Mark 2:27). Christ knew his Father had given the day as a gift of love, not to establish a rigorous legality of privation.

The dramatic dialogue between Christ and the Jewish religious leaders regarding Sabbath reads as though he deliberately and persistently confronted and challenged their corrosive, petrified, insidious Sabbath prejudices. No less than seven Sabbath-healing episodes are reported, besides several controversies about Sabbath-keeping. The stories of miraculous healing constantly evoke themes of liberation, joy, and service—Sabbath concepts which were adamantly grasped by the prophets. He says to one, "Woman you are *freed* from your infirmity."

Christ challenged faulty conceptions of Sabbath. Why? Because God had given this day to his people as a picture in time by which to remember the face of the One who was the Lord of the Sabbath; and now the spiritual leaders of the day were destroying his features.

Christ stood in a synagogue on Sabbath and read the passage from Isaiah which has been termed a nutshell summary of the messianic program:

"The Spirit of the Lord is upon me, because he has anointed me to preach good news to the poor. He has sent me to proclaim release to the captives and recovering of sight to the blind, to set at liberty those who are oppressed, to proclaim the acceptable year of the Lord" (Luke 4:18,19).

Then he closed the book, gave it back to the attendant, sat down, with the eyes of all in the synagogue fixed on him, and he had the audacity to say, "Today this scripture has been fulfilled in your hearing." What he meant was: the messianic promise is now taking place.

Christ announces, "The Son of man is lord of the sabbath" (Luke 6:5). His shout was as loud as the Baptizer's "Get ready!", a companion litany to the wilderness warning. And it rings on, tolling over and over, for those who have ears to hear.

Christ is the crux of Sabbath understanding; he is the Messiah the Jew senses, waits for, and vaguely comprehends in weekly observance—a holy idea stuck in the Judaical religious birth canal. Christ is the One in whom all Sabbath longing and celebration is truly fulfilled, and without whom there is no full Sabbath participation. He is the One who comes close to his church gathered, this new godly idea for modeling the better society; he is the one for whom we set aside a whole twenty-four hour period in our week to enjoy. He is the One for whom we are getting ready.

And looking into Sabbath with its concept of mercy, with its quality of delight, with its gift of time from wearying work, with its perpetual joyful observance, with its celebration of loving union, with its sense of resting from all the agonies that can be bondages to man, with its peace is like looking into the face of One we love, whose eyes engage our own. Christ is the Lord of the Sabbath.

We get ready for his union with us in a special sense this one day each week so that we can better perceive his presence the rest of the days.

We get ready for him weekly so we will be in practice to be ready for him at the nativity of his second coming.

Life is filled with human good-byes, with separations and reunions. We part daily as humans, and then we return to one another. David's homecoming after a workday is accompanied by familiar sounds. From my study, I hear the crunch of tires on gravel, the car door slamming, the front door creaking open, the banging of his briefcase on the old oak dining table, a pause while he checks the mail, then his "halloo—Ho-ho-ho! Guess who's home!" And I know it's been a good day.

When the children come home from college, we get their rooms ready for sleeping and plan special food; we thrust aside the demands of work and ministry; we sit in the living room on the comfortable couch, softening noticeably with the passing years, and we talk, and laugh, and share our lives. We practice welcoming one another back, whether it's from work, school, or a trip. We stop in the middle of dinner preparation and say the words, "It's so good to have you home." We pause to embrace. We inquire, "How was your day?" It is so wonderful to have someone to come home to, and it's wonderful to have someone to come home to us. And sometimes we remember to remind ourselves how terrible it would be if the coming-homes, the reunions, the returns after workdays were no more; if the loved ones never came home again, if the anticipation of waiting was forever over. This thought makes us work harder at the practice of greeting, the habit of welcome, the rituals of home-coming.

Likewise, we must also work at getting ready for Sunday. We cannot worship if our hearts are full of secular responsibilities, bitter anguishes, old guilts, and aching sins. We cannot praise with equanimity if we are harried by unfulfilled commitments, distraught over incomplete promises, unsettled because of the Sunday morning fracas. We must ready ourselves physically. We must ready ourselves spiritually. We must ready ourselves emotionally and psychologically. This takes practice which will at first seem difficult. Establishing new disciplines is always exhausting.

David and I took up playing racquetball because after four babies, I was in terrible physical condition. A right-hander, he nevertheless played with his left hand, gave me two points for every one point I made, and one point for every time I broke his serve. The first game we played, I ran around for ten minutes and spent the next twenty panting in a flushed, overheated heap on the floor while my husband improved his volley.

It took months before I could play for a straight hour, and even then my powder-puff backhand was ridiculous.

But after a while, the discipline of work freed me physically, and I could hold my own (if I got mad enough) at my own game (two points to his one, one point for every broken serve and my good right-hand against his increasingly improved left-hand!). Several times, much to our surprise, I even beat him!

With this same principle in mind while establishing Sunday disciplines, we must anticipate that at first there will be frustrations; getting ready will seem like a lot of work. Initially, we won't see the benefits. We will fail, experience anxiety, huff and puff, wonder where the heightened sense of Christ's presence is.

What we must do is keep practicing. Lower our expectations a little; choose the disciplines that fit our individual style or those acceptable to our family profile. Refuse to be tempted to try everything at once. And keep practicing!

In *Divine Rest for Human Restlessness* (1980, p. 250), Samuel Bacchiocchi tells of the privilege system that governed the social relationship between the sexes in the English school where he attended college. A couple with "A" status was entitled to a weekly meeting of about one hour in a designated lounge. Those couples with a "B" or "C" status could officially meet only bi-weekly or monthly. "Frankly," writes the author, "I did my best to maintain the "A" status because I viewed those weekly encounters with my fiancée, brief as they were, as indispensable for the survival of our relationship." Bacchiocchi learned how to maintain academic preparedness so he would be ready for weekly encounters with his loved one.

Then he goes on to make this point, "The Sabbath is a special weekly encounter with our Creator Redeemer. This encounter lasts not merely one hour but a whole day. It's a sobering thought, that to enter into that holy day means to enter into the spiritual presence and communion of the Lord."

That, I am convinced, is an encounter well worth getting ready for. This coming close, this holy return, this spiritual reunion is well worth the practice of getting ready. In the next three chapters, we will discuss physical preparation, emotional preparation, and spiritual preparation for the Lord's Day.

5

Getting Organized

TWO PRINCIPLES HAVE helped me immensely in my struggle to get physically ready for Sunday.

The first principle is organizational: I try to have all the physical preparations completed for Sunday by Saturday afternoon.

The second principle is motivational: I try to have all the physical preparations readied as though Christ were going to be a special guest in our home.

Ingrid Trobish writes in *Bright Legacy* about her grandmother Johanna Lind Hult, a woman who was widowed at forty-three, with eight children (ranging in age from two to nineteen) to raise on her own. "During the time I lived with her, she taught me that all Saturday work—cleaning, baking, preparations for Sunday—must be finished by noon. This was her unswerving rule. Then, as she told me, 'I go to my bedroom and close the door. My Lord and I have time to fellowship and I study His word.'"

I am not quite up to the standard of Johanna Lind
Hult, but I have discovered that adapting to the weekly
Jewish rhythm of the sacred enhances my organizational
skills. About Wednesday I begin to think, "Ah, Sunday is
coming. How can we continue to make this the high
point of our week?" I check family schedules and make
sure I know who will be traveling, who will be home,
who is forming weekend plans of their own. I take garments to the cleaners, do laundry and make sure Sunday
clothes are ironed and hanging fresh in closets. I make
lists, think about menus, check recipe books and anticipate having guests either on Lord's Day Eve or for Sunday brunch after the early church service.

Housecleaning is reserved for Friday or Saturday
morning. Since I hate the exhaustion from doing laundry, cleaning, errands, grocery shopping, and cooking
all on one day (unless I have a big and cooperative
crew), I try to spread all these responsibilities over the
week. The bedroom house level is cleaned early in the
week with a quick go-over Saturday morning (or a reminder that everyone is to vacuum and pick up their
own room).

The goal is to be physically prepared by some time
Saturday afternoon so that we can begin to ease into
relaxation with the internal satisfaction of work completed, the enjoyment of one another's company, and the
anticipation of the next day—Sunday. To be truthful,
this doesn't always happen as carefully planned; but I
am getting better and better at achieving my goal.

Gerita Garver Liebelt (a Sabbatarian who practices
Sabbath in the Jewish custom from sundown Friday to
sundown Saturday) discusses getting ready physically in
her book *From Dilemma to Delight*. A minister's wife,
she tells of having heard her children say, "I hate Fridays!" (meaning they were tired of all the work they
were asked to do to get ready for Sabbath—all on one
day), and this motivated their mother to reorganize her

work schedule in order to reduce the dread and emphasize the delight. By doing one thing each day of the week in preparation for Sabbath, she figured out a schedule where she could be prepared at the end of the week without feeling too hurried. For example, on Monday she washes the Sabbath clothes, on Tuesday she irons them, on Wednesday she plans the Sabbath menu and the Sabbath day's activities and does the shopping, on Thursday she bakes and prepares food for the Sabbath meals. Then on Friday, she completes the preparation.

For the Mains household, I've found that a little outside help relieves the pressure of Sunday preparation. Our children are young adults, in college, or in high school, and I recognize that the burdens of school activities, homework, and extra responsibilities which they carry are often equal to my own. Consequently, I hire a young teen to give me a hand for a couple of hours by dusting and pushing a vacuum. This is not a large expense, but it takes the edge off my work, frees me from nagging my own busy offspring, and puts pocket money into someone else's jeans. Thus, physical preparation is accomplished without the emotional baggage of coercion, failed expectations, or frustration from forgetfulness.

However, this does not mean that our children are exempt from all preparation responsibilities.

I depend on them to contribute to family readiness by picking-up, running errands, doing yard work, ironing their own clothes and putting away clean laundry, keeping their own rooms in order, lending a hand in the kitchen in food preparation, and in the clearing and washing of dishes. The readiness systems we are devising seem to be working fairly well due to a little extra effort given by outside help.

Every family will devise their own organizational styles with unique divisions of labor that adapt to the ages, abilities, interests, and expectations in each home. But again, the goal of this planning is to be finished and

ready sometime Saturday afternoon so we can anticipate
Sunday with a Sabbath heart.

The Jewish Catalog (a compendium of Jewish practices for the modern Jew) talks about getting ready,
"Shabbat is the crowning glory in the life of the devout
Jew. Countless generations of Jews followed the advice
of Shammai the Elder who, whenever he found some
especially tasty bit of food, would set it aside to be eaten
on Shabbat. Jews who lived in poverty would deprive
themselves all week in order to honor the Sabbath with
light, wine, and proper food."

Learning to think about Sunday around Wednesday or
Thursday is one of the mental organizational tools I now
use as a Christian to make sure that the housework, the
weekday physical preparations don't bleed into the Lord's
Day. (It is also surprising what inward emotional pleasure
this Wednesday thought brings me.)

THE SECOND PRINCIPLE OF PHYSICAL READINESS

*The second principle I use which enhances my physical
readiness is to train myself to think that Christ is going to
be my houseguest*—he will "arrive" sometime Saturday
night and "stay" until Sunday evening. Now the Spirit of
Jesus is with us at all times. I recognize his everyday
immanence as well as his transcendence; but to form a
mental discipline, I get myself and my house ready to
welcome him as a special guest.

The value of this discipline was made clear to me one
Saturday when our small group was scheduled to have
dinner that evening in our home. The week had been
wretched, filled with responsibilities, deadlines, and
unexpected crises. I love the members of our small
group, but very frankly, I was too exhausted to extend
hospitality to anyone and furthermore, I felt like I was

fast coming down with a headcold (which I only catch when I have been under unusual stress).

That morning I prayed the prayer which is becoming my habitual Saturday morning thought, whispered as closely to the moment of waking as possible:

> My Lord Sabbath
> Welcome to my home.
> Welcome to my heart.
> Welcome to my mind.
> Welcome to my spirit.
> May this Sabbath/Sunday
> Be filled with your Presence.
> Amen.

I decided to prepare the meal in *his* honor. I bought a roast, set the table with my best china, picked up flowers for the centerpiece and noticed that about midday my heart was singing. I was thrilled with the thought of serving people I loved, and that evening I was able to honestly greet them with that special inward joy of love, delight, and welcome.

Sabbath and its Lord had come.

In the book *Duchess: The Story of Wallis Warfield Windsor,* by Stephen Birmingham, I was intrigued by a glimpse at the Duchess' style of hospitality. This compulsively organized woman left nothing to chance. Invitations issued by telephone were followed by an engraved card that read: "This is to remind you that the Duke and Duchess of Windsor expect you on Saturday (then the date), for the weekend at teatime."

The guesthouse had two bedrooms and two baths. A female guest was housed in the pink room supplied with pink soap made especially for the Duchess, along with bath salts, medicinal supplies, fresh flowers, and air freshener wrapped in a terry-cloth cover to match the towels.

A male guest was housed in the yellow bedroom decorated with walls of soft felt and matching draperies. His room contained a bar and his bathroom held all the necessary shaving tools with bottles of shaving lotion and cologne arranged with their tops removed.

Guests were expected for tea, and would return to the cottage to rest and dress before dinner. There a male guest would discover that his bags had been completely unpacked, his garments freshly pressed, and his shoes polished. All the drawers and doors were open so that he could see at a glance where each item had been placed. His dress shirt would be laid out, studs in place, handkerchief folded and in the dinner jacket breast pocket, socks turned inside out for the proper toe-first donning. After a black-tie dinner, the guest would retire to his room where he would find a menu card on which he was asked to list what he wished for breakfast and what time he wished to be served. Once filled out, this card was to be placed outside the door to his room.

Breakfast was served in bed: in the pink and white bedroom, on white china with a pink strawberry motif, along with a small vase of pink and white flowers . . . and in the yellow bedroom, on yellow china with yellow flowers.

Well, at least you can say that the Duchess of Windsor knew how to get ready for guests! Frankly, I suspect her brand of hospitality would have left me cold. At any rate it certainly is a far cry from the Mains' style of "wonderful to have you here; please make yourself a part of the family; how about starting with peeling the potatoes!"

I want to be physically prepared, not for physical preparations' sake (which is always a temptation), but so that my heart will be free to welcome.

Scripture teaches that we are to welcome one another as Christ has welcomed us for the glory of God (Romans 15:7), but I think I am learning to welcome Christ as others have welcomed me!

I've jokingly said to David that I could write an article titled, "The Beds I've Slept In"! While traveling in ministry I've been the recipient of varied forms of hospitality and I have slept in many wonderful and strange places. I've slept in an old mahogany four-poster in a parsonage in Jamaica where the hyacinths grew outside the window and where the ceiling fans turned in the languid heat. I've slept in a foldaway hide-a-bed that filled so much of the spare room I had to crawl over it to get to the closet and close it to open the door to the hallway. I've slept in a hotel in Thailand where the room attendants turned down your covers and placed a small orchid on the pillow. I've slept in a rickety sleeper, traveling by train to tour refugee camps, where we had to close our windows against bandits. I've slept in an Iranian-owned hotel in Pakistan during the American hostage crisis. I've slept in a dusty suite, far away from traveling companions and listened to the Muslim call to prayer at four in the morning. I've slept in bombed-out Beirut where my room had no lock on the door and I had to push my dresser in place each night to insure security.

I've slept in missionary homes in Venezuela and Columbia and Kenya, and I've taken cold showers, bathed in tubs in rooms without inner ceilings where I could also listen and contribute to the living room conversation while I bathed! I've gone to bed by kerosene light to the sound of African tribes singing beneath the full equator moon. I've slept in bunkbeds in summer camps and in cots in student dormitories. I've slept in mansions. I've slept in YWCAs and YMCAs! The only place I haven't slept is in a hammock or on a bare dirt floor—and that's probably somewhere in my future!

One home in particular where I was a guest is typical

of the kindness I have received in so many places. And I often think of this special hospitality when preparing my own home for the Lord's Day.

The guest room in this home was beautifully arranged. There was a basket of fresh fruit and interesting reading material by the bedside. Plenty of fluffy towels were in the bathroom and a coverlet was placed on the bed in case I wanted to nap.

Quiet and privacy were provided to rest from traveling and to prepare myself to speak in the evening session; yet all the while, one of the daughters, a concert pianist, practiced classical music on the grand piano downstairs. I began to feel my body and soul and mind relax.

The next morning the breakfast table was set with welcoming fresh linens. We drank grape juice from backyard vines and spread homemade jellies on the toast. Saturday evening dinner was a dining-room affair served on old family china. The food was mostly homegrown— even the salmon had been caught by the husband—and all was lovingly prepared.

It was a joy being in that home, among those people. There was obviously a spiritual gift of love at work. Not only did this strengthen me for the ministry of the days ahead, but I came home vowing to be a better homemaker myself, promising myself to take more pains with my hostessing—not to be so busy that small details are overlooked. I especially try to remember this when I prepare to welcome the Lord on Sunday, and other Sunday guests who bring their own special blessing when they share the Lord's Day with us.

How wonderful it would be to have welcomed Christ to my home when he was physically on this earth! The gospel is full of references to people who had just such a privilege. Mary and Martha and Lazarus' home in Bethany seemed to have been a kind of headquarters for Jesus and his fellow workers when they were in the

Jerusalem area. What miracles they were all witness to when Christ was present!

On one Sabbath, Scripture says, "he left the synagogue, and entered the house of Simon and Andrew. . . . Now Simon's mother-in-law lay sick with a fever, . . . And he came and took her by the hand and lifted her up and the fever left her; and she served them" (Mark 1:29–31).

Levi, the tax collector (called to be the apostle Matthew) makes a great feast in his house for Christ and includes all his buddies—publicans and sinners. Christ invited himself to Zacchaeus' house and that little man was never the same. In fact few of the people whose homes Jesus entered were unaltered. They were either infuriated with him or transformed.

Phrases like "when he went into the house" and "he was dining at the house of" and "he was in the house of" pepper the gospel accounts. Homes were places of meeting and entertaining, of dining and conversation. They were also centers of ministry. Christ instructed the twelve on their mission of preaching and healing, "And whatever house you enter, stay there, and from there depart."

Christ also taught, "He who receives you receives me, and he who receives me receives him who sent me" (Matthew 10:40).

I am learning to get ready for the Lord's Day, to get my home ready to greet Christ, to welcome him or to welcome those who represent him; I am preparing myself to be hospitable in a way that is different from what I am able to be during the rest of the week when work harries me and deadlines loom and schedules march across our calendars.

Amazing things occur when Christ is present. The hostess rises from her sick-bed, healed; minds are challenged; sins forgiven. The emotions are freed for weeping, for laughter. We touch and are touched. The very walls of the rooms seem to bend to listen. The candles burn brighter. The new day rises more hopefully. The sun smiles.

I rise on Saturday thinking—only a few more things to make ready: early-morning shopping, the tables to be set for company, get one of the boys to stir up a box cake.

He is coming! He is coming!

We need new candles, one more load of laundry. Time for morning prayers.

We are almost ready! Christ is coming!

At last, ready and waiting!

Welcome, my Lord. Welcome to my home on this Lord's Day Eve.

On Saturdays I open the doors of my home and my heart with a deeply felt welcome to my Lord, and Sundays have never been so special!

6

Getting
Rid of Sunday
Anxieties

AN INSECURE LITTLE character called Binkley in
the nationally syndicated cartoon strip, *Bloom County*
by Burke Breathed, represents the child in all of us who
feels like he's the butt of all the world's humiliations.

One of the regular features is a cartoon panel with
Binkley sitting up in bed facing his closet. "Pst, Binkley,
over here," says a voice from out of sight. Then a horri-
ble rhino-nosed monster sticks his face out of the closet
and says, "On behalf of myself and the rest of your sub-
conscious anxieties we thought you should be given ad-
vance notice regarding our plan to jump out and grab
you this evening."

"Thank you," says Binkley.

"Certainly," says the monster.

The last panel shows Binkley hunched beneath the
blanket with a baseball bat in hand. The closet door is

closed, and Binkley says, "A closet full of courteous anxieties is a dubious comfort."

It's terrible to be a child and have a closet full of anxieties.

It's even more terrible to be an adult with a closet full of anxieties; and I suspect that for many Christian adults, going to church on Sunday morning is like opening Binkley's door filled with monsters and Minotaurs, creatures and creepies, bugs and bears and bats and other pieces of personal whimsy.

For many of us something has gone wrong with Sunday morning. It's become filled with too many monsters: the late-arrival panic monster, the waiting Minotaur of too many responsibilities, the creeping creature of inner-fraternal hostilities or resentments or hatreds. This church closet is haunted with dull sermons and boring services. There is often a whole choir of voices singing the hymn, "You're not what you're supposed to be." Or how about the all-too-familiar anthem, "You'll never make it as a good Christian"?

One leaves church all too frequently Sunday after Sunday having peered into the closet full of anxieties, but never having truly exorcised the monsters who inhabit its dark territories. "Good," we think, "another Sunday behind us. Don't have to face that again for a whole week! Am I relieved!" And we leave, having no idea that we've just participated in a form of godliness without the power of godliness; that our Sunday attendance has been perfunctory, without meaning; an intellectual exercise in neutral without ever shifting into the high gear of heart and soul beating upward toward worship.

No wonder people stop going to church or their attendance becomes irregular. Any excuse, any excuse whatsoever—a slight cold, overdue homework, too much weekend paper work—becomes reason enough to stay away, and we sigh to ourselves and say, "I don't get anything out of it anyway."

What we need to undergo is an emotional and psychological closet-cleaning. We need to face into the dark of all those churchly anxieties, instead of just letting them lurk in the shadows robbing us of our rightful Sunday enthusiasm. Like Binkley, we need to take baseball bat in hand and get rid of them.

For years the big question in our home was: Why did our family equilibrium tilt precariously out of control between Saturday night and Sunday morning?

One child would be missing a crucial dress item that I had overlooked in the back of a closet. This precipitated a quick wash and dry, then ironing out the damp fabric on the ironing board. It seemed even the dog collaborated with confusion, invariably vomiting on the living room carpet.

There was never toothpaste in the right bathroom, there were the usual my-turn-first arguments—to use the blowdryer, to take a shower, ad infinitum. And about a half an hour before departure time for church, this overwhelming panic would begin to rise from the pit of my stomach, constrict my chest, and finally explode from my mouth, "Let's get going! We're going to be late! Haven't you had your breakfast yet? Why do we have to go through this every Sunday? No, your shirt isn't ironed—I'm getting it; I'm getting it. I don't know where you left your Bible! Why does everybody think I'm responsible when they lose things? We're going to be late. Let's go. Come on! Out the door!"

I turned into Alice's white rabbit in the crazy wonderland of Sunday morning, "We're late; we're late, for a very important date—" and looking back, I suspect there were some members of my family who thought I turned into the Wicked Witch of the West every Lord's Day.

Actually, I was living out an unintentional lie, an unconscious untruth that develops due to many factors, one of which may be a family system in which we simply

accept fiction for being fact. The vital lie I was creating
stated: Sunday is the worst day of the week.

This was an untruth that hid itself in my heart even
through those years when a major effort of our pastoral
ministry was to create new forms of meaningful contemporary worship. And this fiction hid itself in my heart
even though David and I had been working hard at creating a satisfactory form of Sunday family celebration. For
years, we'd begun to get ready for Sunday morning on
Saturday evening. We'd made physical preparations—
clothes ready and lessons done and a peaceful house.
We'd made spiritual preparations, time for prayer, time
for meditation. But I still experienced the old, rising
panic, the white rabbit sing-song, "We're late; we're
late!", the gut-level churning, the Sunday morning anxiety attack.

I've since learned that Christians must make psychological preparations for Sunday morning as well as
physical preparations if they're going to destroy the
old, unintentional lie: Sunday is the worst day of the
week.

David Seamond's book *Putting Away Childish Things*
deals with the influence of the unhealed child of the
past on the adult of the present. While reading this, the
Holy Spirit brought to mind my barely controllable
panic on Sunday mornings. I heard my husband's voice
saying, "Why are you so upset? We have plenty of time."
I thought of the kids complaining, "Mo-om, why are you
in such a frit? I can make it by the time we need to
leave." In prayer, I said, "Lord, show me why Sunday
mornings are such a bad time for me."

Then I thought back to *my* childhood Sunday mornings, back to that house beneath its bending elms.
Because Dad was the music minister in most of the
churches we attended when I was a child, Sunday morning choir practices, the morning worship service, youth
choir at four in the afternoon, and the evening service

all fell into his capable hands; but these tasks also spelled a very full day.

Both my parents worked during the week, so Saturday was the day we attempted to complete all the household responsibilities that hadn't been finished. My parents' lives were crowded with people and family and students—my father giving private voice lessons in the living room on Saturday mornings and my mother making remarkable plans for her grand Sunday dinner. Consequently, Sunday mornings in my childhood home were also crammed with everything that didn't get done on Saturday to get us ready for Sunday morning.

Invariably, my brother or sister lost a shoe. I don't know why it was shoes particularly, but it always was. And keys were another thing that always seemed to disappear, necessitating a last-minute panicked hunt. With Mother in the kitchen putting her glorious Sunday cuisine together, a lot of the responsibility for herding siblings into clothes and sniffing out lost items fell to the oldest child. Guess who? You guessed right. Me.

The light dawned. My Sunday panic that was creating a fiction for me and my family that Sunday was the worst day of the week was nothing more than an old pattern, an unwelcome remnant from childhood. Even as an adult, I was acting out what every Sunday morning in my youthful life had been. In fact, the vital lie I'd been creating was threatening to become real. *Sunday morning was the worst day in our family life because I was making it the worst day!*

Some of the fictions in our lives don't burgeon from deep emotional need. They simply come from old patterns we need to discard for newer and holier ones. We must learn to ask: Why am I behaving the way I'm behaving, and what does it remind me of?

My parents were wonderful people—but they did have a tendency to rush at life, and they needed to discover the calm presence of the real Christ on Sunday mornings.

Many people have had childhood Sunday mornings like
mine and must recognize that the old inward panic experienced Sunday after Sunday is an outworn habit.

I've discarded this childhood leftover by first of all
anticipating that my habit is going to act up on Sunday
mornings. I'm kind to the little child within still beginning to panic. I make warm noises—*now, now, you're
going to be all right.* I mother, nurture, console my inner
self—*you don't need to worry, everything's under control, take some deep breaths; I really am in charge and
all is well.* Very infrequently, I might chide, *Oh, just
grow up!* One of these self-parenting techniques invariably works like a charm.

Some of us come from backgrounds where a restrictive, narrow, confining legalism squeezed the life, the
holy life, out of the Lord's Day.

Perhaps you were raised in this kind of Lord's Day
tradition. A friend told me about Sundays when she was
a girl. She and her sister were forbidden to play; but they
found a way around the restriction when they discovered
they could walk on the beach if they passed out gospel
tracts. She was aware, however, of the incongruity of her
attire—patent leather Mary Janes and frilly Sunday
school dresses. Her conclusion was: "I hated Sundays."
You may need to forgive those who pressed upon the
moist dough of your once young soul the sharp-edged
cookie cutter mold of legalism.

You too may be living in a fiction that says: Sunday is
the worst day of the week. My prayer for you is that you
will not discard Sunday, but that you will instead discard
the old negative legalism in order to rediscover the delight of which the prophets speak. My prayer for you is
that you will suddenly confront the truth that Sunday
can be the best of all times, a celebration of the Christ
who is in the midst of us.

Since a Sunday spirit, either negative or positive, can
be caught, it behooves parents to be careful what kind

of Sunday experience they are modeling. Some church-going lifestyles seem deliberately designed to spoil a child's inner emotional response to this special day. If we had intentionally decided to make the Lord's Day onerous, we couldn't be doing a better job. Do you rush and push and shout and become generally unpleasant on Sunday mornings? Do you complain about church? Are you sloppy in your attendance? Or are you over-conscientious about matters that are not really important? Are you compulsive about church attire, about Sunday good behavior? Do you always negate the pastor, the choir, the length of services, the usher crew, etc.?

Then don't be surprised if your children grow up to look at Sunday as the worst day of the week.

George Gallup, Jr., the national pollster, warns that the youngest adults—those just growing out of their teenage years, some still living in their parents' Christian home—represent the least Christian segment of our population. If this is so, something has gone wrong in the Christian homes of our country, in the spiritual nurturing of our own children.

In an article entitled "There's Nothing Wrong with Hand-Me-Down Faith" (*Moody Monthly,* June 1976), pastor Ray Stedman concentrates on a phrase from Deuteronomy 6: "and you shall teach them diligently to your children." Then he writes to parents, "Notice that you shall teach. Like many licenses, this one should be stamped 'non-transferable.' The Sunday School and church cannot substitute for parents in teaching spiritual truth. Only parents have the time, the concern, and the relationship with their children to make it work. No one has as much influence on children as parents. Therefore, God holds parents responsible to teach their children how to love him with all their hearts, and souls, and might."

It is safe to conclude that if you are expecting Sunday school teachers to develop in your children a long-lasting regard for the whole Sunday experience, you are expecting too much from one hour a week. What happens in your home, the emotional tone you as a parent are establishing, your own inner attitude toward Sunday which is "caught" will be the strongest factor in determining whether your child one day abandons Sunday observance.

The late Dr. Donald Grey Barnhouse, for years the radio voice of "The Bible Study Hour," was once asked the question: "At what age can a child understand what it means to love God?" His response was: "You begin teaching a child about God twenty years before he's born."

He meant that the initial instruction about God grows out of the character of the parent. We cannot give to our children a spiritual life we ourselves do not possess. In a *Christianity Today Institute* on teaching children spiritual truth, Wes Willis, a Christian educator stated, ". . . the healthy Christian development of a child is tied to the continuing development of the parent." And Donald Joy, a professor of human development at Asbury Theological Seminary says, "Fathers and mothers, just in the business of doing their parenting, are unwittingly the first curriculum for representing God."

A parent is the primary forceful model for developing a rich inner Sunday appreciation in his/her child. Therefore, it is imperative that we as parents come to terms with our own outworn childish Sunday attitudes so that we don't create a closet full of Sunday anxieties for our children.

Nor is it enough to take a laissez-faire attitude, a live-and-let-live philosophy toward Sunday in which there is no deliberately established concept regarding Lord's Day observance given to our children as part of their spiritual inheritance. Sociological studies on dysfunctional families provide some insight at this point.

Children who are severely beaten or even murdered at the hands of their parents are the focus of media coverage nearly every day. This attention to the dramatic cases has resulted in the public equating child maltreatment with physical abuse. Child social workers, however, know that there is another, hidden form of abuse which has been virtually ignored despite the fact that it is reported to authorities more frequently and accounts for more deaths than physical violence.

The cause of that kind of abuse is simply parental neglect.

According to statistics from the National Study on Child Neglect and Abuse Reporting, only four out of every one hundred reported children experienced a type of major physical injury, whereas sixty out of every one hundred reported children experienced a type of physical neglect. Furthermore, whereas major physical injury was associated with 34 percent of child deaths reported in 1981, neglect was associated with 56 percent.

Neglect includes emotional, physical, nutritional, and psychological deprivations. The neglectful parent is one who is careless about nurturing, who is ill-equipped to protect and who has little, if next to no, parenting skills, often having been raised himself in a neglectful family.

Not surprisingly, the children from these families displayed negative behaviors nearly 50 percent more often than the children in control families. Neglected children as a group scored significantly lower than their peers in nearly all developmental areas. Neglected children generally scored lower even than abused children. The greatest deficits were found in the area of language development, although behavior problems were noted by researchers. For example, neglected children wiggled, fiddled, interrupted, teased, cried and whined, were easily distracted, and had intense emotional responses and tantrums. They fought, and were both physically and verbally aggressive. They were defiant while at the same time demanding excessive amounts of adult attention; they destroyed objects on purpose, told lies, were fearful, often moody, and took an "I can't" approach to tasks.

The list goes on, but the analogy that needs to be drawn from this sociological information is this: This Christian generation is guilty of a type of neglect which results in spiritual impoverishment. We are not teaching our children how to keep the Sabbath holy. Many of us have abandoned an old restrictive legalism, but we have not replaced it with a joyful holy celebration. If Sunday is not a day that is so special that we and our children look forward to it with delight, then we are neglectful parents.

Psalm 78:5–7 declares, "[God] established a testimony in Jacob, and appointed a law in Israel, which he commanded our fathers to teach to their children; that the next generation might know them, the children yet unborn, and arise and tell them to their children, so that they should set their hope in God, and not forget the works of God, but keep his commandments." Christianity is always only a generation away from extinction.

We must teach spiritual truths to our children, not depend upon someone else to do it. More than this, we must model in our own homes that we are becoming spiritual people. Our attitude toward all of God's commandments, our obedience to them can't help but be absorbed by those offspring in our own home. And what better way to start than linking Lord's Day observance to the Sabbath principle; this is close to God's heart.

If we neglect to make Sundays special in our homes, we must not shake our heads one day when we discover that we have raised children who are spiritually wiggly; who cry and whine and are distracted from things of the soul; who develop intense emotional dislikes regarding church; who are defiant toward those very things we hold dear; whose greatest deficiency is the inability to love God with all their heart, mind, and strength; who have become part of a statistical population segment known as those who have fallen away from Christianity. We have simply raised children suffering from the effects of childhood spiritual neglect.

To prevent this from happening in the next generation, and in the next, we must open our own closet full of anxieties, shine a light within, pull out the stacks of old attitudes and prejudices; throw away the outgrown garments, now moth-eaten and unwearable, of a past season; junk the broken leftovers, now unusable. We must undergo some renovation—fresh paint, tidy organizers to hang and store new ideas. We must make that church closet a joy to peer into, a storage center that causes inward satisfaction because of its order, its neatness, its careful cleanliness.

It must be so clean that when strangers come, or guests, or our own families and open the door, nothing unseemly will tumble out. Emotionally we will have become Sunday ready.

7

Getting
Heart and Mind
Ready

ESAU TRADED HIS BIRTHRIGHT for a bowl of pottage. A steamy bowl of thick soup to fill a hungry stomach might be a good bargain under certain conditions; but to cavalierly yield the rights of the firstborn, the spiritual authority invested in such a position, the opportunity to be included among the catalog of patriarchs reiterated throughout the ages . . . Abraham, Isaac, and *Esau*—that was a bitter exchange no matter how savory the lentil stew! The loss was unredeemable; forever after the roll of patriarchal names would be Abraham, Isaac, and *Jacob*.

What about we Christians today? Are we trading our spiritual birthright?

Psalm 105 says, "Let the hearts of those who seek the Lord rejoice! Seek the Lord and his strength, seek his presence continually!"; Psalm 95, "Let us come into his presence with thanksgiving"; Psalm 16, "in thy

presence there is fulness of joy." This magnificent privilege, knowing the presence of God in church each Sunday morning, which is by rights that of the believer
should not be bartered for appetizers with empty calo-
ries; but many Christians today are exchanging this
spiritual birthright for the meager fare of lesser treats.

SET ASIDE THINGS THAT DISTRACT

Often people are not spiritually prepared to experience Christ's presence in church because they have
sated their hunger with whatever is featured on the TV
menu on Saturday night. Please don't misunderstand.
These people don't skip church on Sunday morning because they watched TV into the wee hours. No, they
were in church—at least, their bodies were—and they
listened politely, even if passively. However, there was
no sense of anticipation regarding the service, no excitement that Christ would speak to them, no talking about
the service afterward with friends and family.

A vital question we need to ask ourselves regarding
our Sunday observance is: *Do I really experience the
presence of Christ in church?*

One of the reasons for our spiritual dehydration on
Sundays—one of the reasons the Lord's Day seems routine, involving nothing supernatural—is that we often
have a difficult time focusing on the subject at hand. For
many this means their minds keep flashing back to
scenes from the movie they watched the night before
(whether G or R rated), or to a Saturday night TV program (network or cable, squeaky clean or filthy dirty),
or to the interesting book they stayed up to read. Still
others have their minds on some sports event they
attended on Saturday night. Instead of meditating on
the Cross, or Communion, or Scripture, their brain is
plugged into the events of the previous night.

And Christians rarely feel guilt or sorrow over such intrusive thoughts, hardly realizing that hymns and prayer and Communion have become a cultural experience rather than a spiritual encounter or that a spiritual infidelity is being committed. Many have become more like Esau than they realize. They are trading spiritual priorities for a bowl of soup. Hebrews 12:16 says that Esau was immoral and irreligious because he "sold his birthright for a single meal." When week after week we are cheated in similar barters, will not God accuse us of the same?

What am I saying? Is it wrong to watch TV on Saturday night, or go to a ball game, spend three or four hours reading a novel, or just have a good time socializing Saturday night with friends? No. But it might be advisable to choose other times for these activities if they interfere with your ability to experience the presence of Christ in his church on Sunday morning.

Answer this question as honestly as possible: Do you experience Christ's presence in church Sunday after Sunday?

Accounting for human variables, I know it's hard for me to concentrate on Christ with spiritual sensitivity on Sunday if my mind hasn't been prepared properly on Saturday evening. In quiet and prayer, I focus my thoughts on going to church as a highlight for me, one of the best of times. I dare not miss it. I think of the many Christians in this world who do not have the privilege of church attendance. I resolve to go to church rested, early, and in a spirit of excited anticipation. The living Lord will be there, and through adoration, through inner communion, through the sacraments or symbols of the Last Supper, we will establish a deep union.

Thousands of cards which read: **Pre-empted for spiritual prime time** were printed for listeners to our national radio ministry (see sample, p.111). At one end there's a hole in the middle so it can fit over a TV knob. (It can also be slipped into a book as a place marker.) For many it serves as an effective reminder to at least experiment with setting aside prime time for spiritual preparation.

This card is simply a Saturday evening reminder that something far better than this tasty TV stew is being offered in the morning. Hanging on the knob of the television set, it says: "Don't spoil your appetite for spiritual feasting by gorging on junk food with no comparative nutritional value."

Preparation is the key if we are to restore Sunday to the kind of day God intends for it to be. Proper Saturday evening preparation readies one for the magnificent privilege of experiencing Christ's presence each Sunday morning. Therefore, we must be cautious with what we nourish our minds and spirit if we are to be spiritually active, attentive, and receptive the next day.

When Christians consistently fail to experience the presence of Christ on Sunday, they dry up spiritually. They dehydrate.

One of the most dreaded diseases throughout time has been the deadly cholera. Highly contagious, cholera bacteria are transmitted in food and water and by flies. John Masters writes about a cholera epidemic in 1856 in a novel about Bengal:

> They came in, carried or supported by their relatives and lay down . . . they voided their bowels where they lay . . . they gulped thirstily and, a minute later, would vomit up what they had drunk. They shrank as the substance was drawn from every part of the body. Noses became pointed . . . skin wrinkled and had no resilience. When those signs came, they had neither fear of death nor will to live.

Strangely enough, the cholera victim doesn't die so much from the general body poisoning caused by the disease as much as from the shock of drastic dehydration. Dehydration has been a killer throughout the centuries. Hundreds of thousands have died as their bodies simply dried out.

Until the rise of modern medicine, nothing could be done for these victims. Then intravenous feedings began to miraculously restore lost fluid content in a body until a disease like cholera had run its course. But in areas where no modern equipment is available, thousands could still die in an epidemic before health organizations could rush emergency equipment and health professionals to the scene of the outbreak.

Very recently, however, another simple solution is saving thousands of lives. It requires no complicated modern technology, no trained experts and uses elements available in nearly every culture. This solution is called *oral rehydration therapy.* That simply means that a mixture of water, salt, and sugar is administered by mouth to the victim whose suffering body is able to tolerate this uncomplicated solution which quickly replaces the water, sodium, and bicarbonate lost through disease dehydration. Today thousands of lives are being saved by this simple process of oral rehydration.

It's amazing to me how often the simplest of ideas has the most powerful effects!

In a sense, we might make an application to the state of the North American church; we might say that in some places the church is suffering from a problem of dehydration brought on by an acute epidemic of spiritual ennui.

Oh, I'm not saying that there isn't church growth, that converts aren't coming to know the Lord, that new programs aren't being devised and new buildings being built, or that numerous parachurch organizations aren't springing up overnight. But it seems to me that many of us Christians who want to do the work of the Lord are suffering from a strange malady of spiritual dryness. And this particular dehydration, this shriveling of the juices of life, I would call *the disease of lack of spiritual power.* We are a busy church. We are an active church. In many places we are a full church—nonetheless, we seem to be a church without power.

I say this in contrast to the great cloud of darkness which is rising over our nation and enfolding us in its shadows—the insatiable child pornography industry, family violence, x-rated video cassettes to show in the privacy of the home, Christian leaders who succumb to the sexual temptations of our times. Why is the church without the spiritual strength to combat the demonic forces of our age in order that the light of Christianity might prevail?

How frequently do strangers and sojourners enter our sanctuaries because they are drawn by an unexplainable sense of something remarkable? How often do people experience healing (physical and psychological and spiritual) because they attended a Sunday morning service—because they simply sat in a pew? How many times does the Holy Spirit break through our complacency, convicting us of our sin before God and producing tears and weeping and confession? How many times do we linger in quiet after a service is over just because the presence of Christ is so real we simply want to stay longer in his company? How many times are we stirred in our souls by the Scripture readings included in the liturgy?

When does church attendance become more than an activity? When does it begin to shake us to the very depths of our being?

How often do we cancel attractive weekend plans because we don't want to miss what's happening at our local worship service? How often do we so eagerly look forward to church that we are in our pews at least fifteen minutes early? How often is the spiritual element so appealing that we bring friends and family and neighbors and acquaintances with us? How often do we think, on Monday and Tuesday and Wednesday, about the rich spiritual satisfaction we received from time with God's people on Sunday morning?

SPIRITUAL REHYDRATION THROUGH PRAYER

For the most part, we are a dehydrated church, but there is a simple solution to our dehydration, to our lack of spiritual power—a solution which does not need the technological wizardry of our modern age. That rehydration therapy is prayer—we need to become a praying church again.

Think of Sunday. Think of the amount of work that goes on in preparation for Sunday in the average church. Think of the custodial cleaning. Think of bulletins being typed and duplicated. Think of sermon preparation, of choir practices, of church-school lessons being prepared. Think of freshly laundered altar cloths, of pressed vestments; of the provision of elements for Communion and candles. Think of people arranging flowers for the retables. Think of the gallons of coffee brewed and sweets baked for fellowship hours. Think of the preparation in individual homes; think of clothes being washed and shoes being polished and Bible lessons being studied. . . . Then, think of this: In the midst of all this enormous activity, who has spent five minutes in prayer preparation?

Who is praying for your church? Which of us is devoting a portion of our Saturday by giving fifteen minutes or a half-hour to requesting that the presence of God will so richly manifest himself in our congregation on Sundays that miracles (large and small) will take place as a matter of course?

I suspect not many in any of the congregations of this land do. I know that I am repenting of not praying this way for my church. No wonder we're in a state of spiritual dehydration! No wonder we have an increasing multiplication of programs but an increasing division of power.

I've been reading through Isaiah recently and writing down the promises of watering. "Shower, O heavens, from above, and let the skies rain down righteousness; let the earth open that salvation may sprout forth" (Isaiah 45:8). This is the kind of spiritual rainstorm the churches in our nation need to receive.

David, my husband, has been a lifelong student of those times in the history of God's people when heavenly rehydration brought life again to the drought-cracked souls of men and women. In theological parlance, these times have been called revival; but that word often evokes sweaty-faced preachers going hard after converts during a two-week meeting. Revival, in its classic sense, is when the church comes alive again; when the dried up skin, tissue, muscles, inner organs are again flushed with the fluids of life.

This only happens corporately when church people give themselves to prayer.

In 1794, twenty-three New England ministers, concerned about the spiritual condition of their country, met to consider the question, "What shall we do?" They agreed that revival of the church was badly needed and that prayer was the only means left to them. They issued a "circular letter" asking people to pray for revival, "public prayer and praise . . . on every first Tuesday, of the four quarters of the year, beginning with the first Tuesday of January, 1795, at two o'clock in the afternoon . . . and so continuing from quarter to quarter, and from year to year, until, the good providence of God prospering our endeavors, we shall obtain the blessing for which we pray."

All over the country little praying bands sprang up, "covenants" entered into by Christian people to spend one whole day each month in prayer, "Aaron and Hur Societies" which formed to "hold up the hands of their ministers" through intercession. What happened as a result of this concerted prayer was the most sweeping revival our country has ever known—the Second Great Awakening in the early 1800s.

When David studied this, he too took a vow before God and for more than a decade has been faithfully praying a half hour each Saturday night and Sunday morning for our minister, the local church where we worship, for the churches of this country, for a sweeping spiritual renaissance in our nation.

David's faithful praying is one of the reasons our family is understanding the Lord's Day more fully. It is the spiritual undergirding God has used to create in us a hunger for deeper Sunday meaning.

What is needed to rehydrate a church on the national level is also what is needed to rehydrate us on local levels; and it is as basic a technique as oral rehydration for cholera victims. Simply, we need to learn to pray for our churches.

I am learning to pray for longer periods of time by taking my prayer notebook and sitting before the Lord, then asking him, "Lord, how do you want me to pray?" I have learned I am not doing this alone but joining myself in a small but faithful network of spiritual intercessors, many unknown to me or unmet by me; yet we are joined spiritually in a prayer work to make Sunday worship more meaningful. Then, when thoughts come to my mind, *Pray for your pastor, that he will deliver the Lord's words this Sunday; pray for physical and spiritual protection for his family* —I pray and write these prayers down.

Then I'm silent again, listening. When more thoughts come to mind regarding prayer for the Sunday service and for those participating, I write these down. When I think of nothing else, I move to the next topic, often my own spiritual needs. *Confess your own sins of deed and attitude so that you will have nothing that prohibits your ability to worship.* I do so, write these down and move on always inquiring, "Lord, how is it you want me to pray?"

When we seek rehydration for our parched souls through prayer, the Lord will bless us. "When the poor and needy seek water, and there is none, and their tongue is parched with thirst, I the Lord will answer them . . . I will open rivers on the bare heights, and fountains in the midst of the valleys; I will make the wilderness a pool of water, and the dry land springs of water" (Isaiah 41:17,18).

Oh, how we need this rehydration therapy; we need to be a church of moral influence in our nation again. In *Revivalism and Social Reform* (1965, p. 36) Timothy Smith writes about the church during periods of revival, "Clergymen inspired the dominant social movement of the period, the crusade for humanitarian reform, at every stage. They were the principal arbiters of manners and morals and the most venerated citizens of every community." This kind of influence is the evidence of spiritual power in the church, a power that was unleashed because God's Spirit was freed to work among his people, a power that can only come because God's people have given themselves to prayer. It was a church that was fully rehydrated.

Lord, teach me to expand my feeble prayer for my church and for my own Sunday participation from five minutes to ten, then from ten to twenty. Open the rivers on the bare heights, and in the wilderness pools and springs of water in our dry lands. Amen.

In order to be truly prepared to worship on Sunday morning:

- I must be mentally alert, having put aside all things that distract my mind from spiritual thoughts.
- I must be spiritually in tune, having spent a good and satisfactory time in prayer.

8

Getting-Started
Exercises

NOT LONG AGO I was one of several dinner guests in
the home of a young couple who were in charge of the
planning committee for their church. Over dinner we
began to discuss ideas for meaningful worship services,
but the conversation veered when the wife suddenly
asked, "How do you make Sunday morning better? We
rush around here, reduced to yelling and screaming.
We let the kids out of the car and run into church to be
ready to lead worship, putting on a false front as we go.
Last week, even our worship leader said, 'Let's pray!
I have no business being here with the attitude that I
have!' Why is Sunday always the worst day of the week!"

The other guests at the table nodded their heads in
agreement. It was clear that they understood her experience perfectly. One of them said, "There are often Sundays my husband and I drive to church without saying a
word, we're so mad at each other."

My hostess volunteered an idea, "I know I should have everything ready by Saturday. I am learning about that."

I agreed and then added, "I think you may find it more helpful if you begin to think about Sunday in the old Jewish pattern, that is, to begin to get ready on Wednesday or Thursday." Then I explained about the rhythm of the sacred and what a difference it had made in the Mains' family observance of the Lord's Day.

My host at the head of the table groaned and commented, "What you're talking about means an entire lifestyle change!"

Again, I had to agree, but I went on to assure him and the others that it takes time to change one's system of preparedness for Sunday, to integrate it into the very fabric of weekly living. I explained that David and I had experienced a lot of false starts, that we had learned through trial and error, and that the adaptation had taken us ten years.

At this point, like my host, you may be thinking: This is too much work. So to help you get started, this chapter contains four getting-ready tools that will make developing your own system for Sunday celebration a lot easier than you think. These are helps David and I developed to assist ourselves and our radio audience in physical, mental, emotional, and spiritual preparedness. Taken as a whole, it may seem like a quantity of material, but each idea on its own is simple, requires minimal amounts of time and can be surprisingly effective. Consequently, David and I strongly advise you to choose simple activities; incorporate them slowly, layer by layer—first into your personal life, then your life as a couple (if you are married), then your family life, and finally, you will begin to influence those in your church. But remember, biting off too large a chunk will insure some failures and might discourage you from further efforts.

At the end of this chapter, you will find a calendar

with Sunday in the middle of the week (an exercise that visually encourages you to make the Lord's Day the high point), ten simple exercises from which you can choose one a week to prepare your heart for Sunday, a check-off chart that helps you to be ready to recognize Christ's presence in church each Sunday, and a sample of the **Pre-empted for Spiritual Prime Time** card so you can make your own.

After you have used these to stimulate preparation disciplines, you will probably want to design your own readiness procedures that fit your own preferences, style of organization, and work habits; but these getting-ready tools should be an aid at the beginning of your efforts to turn your week—and your life—around.

In order to put "total change of lifestyle" into a larger perspective, it is good to remind ourselves that though we improve spiritually on a personal and private level, we never live our lives unto ourselves. Our spiritual becoming always influences others—friends, spouses, working acquaintances, extended family, children. One life, spiritually alive, can have profound effect.

To illustrate what I mean, let's take a look at what historian Barbara Tuchman in her book *A Distant Mirror*, calls a century "born to woe"—the calamitous fourteenth century. During this time, from 1300 to 1400, Europe was weakened both physically and morally as a result of the Black Plague and constant wars and uprisings.

Even the church was spiritually bankrupt. This was the time of the Great Schism with a papacy in France at Avignon and another in Rome. These popes—successors, as Petrarch noted, of "The poor fishermen of Galilee"— were now loaded with gold and clad in purple.

Clement VI, a lover of luxury who had 1,080 ermine skins in his personal wardrobe, fed his guests from gold and silver plates and seated them beneath Flemish tapestries and hangings of silk. Receptions for visiting

princes and envoys rivaled the splendors of any secular
court. Papal entertainments, fetes, even tournaments and
balls, reproduced the secular. "I am living in the Babylon
of the West," wrote Petrarch in the 1340s "where
prelates feast at licentious banquets and ride on snowhite
horses decked in gold, fed on gold, soon to be shod in
gold if the Lord does not check this slavish luxury."

The money to support all this grandeur came from spiritual extortion with each level of ecclesiastical hierarchy
taxing the one beneath it until eventually it reached the
common people. From bishops to canons to priors to
priesthood and cloistered clergy, down to mendicant fri-
ars and pardoners, then to plain folk. The pardoners
would sell absolution for any sin from gluttony to homi-
cide, cancel any vow of chastity or fasting, remit any
penance for money. When commissioned by the church
to raise money for a crusade they took from the poor,
peddling salvation and taking advantage of the people's
need and credulity.

Priests who could not read or who in ignorance, stum-
bled through the ritual of the Eucharist were another
scandal as well as those who were notorious as seducers
of women. In the beginning of the next century Pope
John XXIII was deposed on charges of piracy, murder,
rape, sodomy, and incest. (And in one of the most incredible acts of human penance, a contemporary pope
chose this same name in order to redeem and rectify the
actions of his predecessor!—consequently there are two
John XXIIIs in the roll call of history.)

No wonder Barbara Tuchman calls the fourteenth century, the one "born to woe." Yet even in the midst of all
this medieval darkness, a faint light began to shine,
burning on the English shore: "Seen through the tele-
scope of history, he was the most significant Englishman
of his time," writes Tuchman about John Wycliff, an
Oxford theologian and preacher, turned reformer. The
Bible, Wycliff was convinced, had been conceived in

God's mind before the Creation and was therefore entirely true. "No man is so rude a scholar," he said, "but that he may learn the words of the gospel according to his simplicity."

Because of this man's influence the Bible was translated into the common language of the English people. And this small flame that burned on England's shores during a calamitous century became a mighty conflagration in the next century when other reformers began to look into the powerful Word of God for themselves. The Waldensians, the Lollards, the Hussites, the Taborites, the Czech Brethren were all early lights which finally gave way to Luther in the sixteenth century and after him Zwingli and Calvin, then the Anabaptists and the free church movements, the Moravians, the Mennonites, not to mention Catholic reformers—all men and women who took the Scripture at face value and allowed it to purify their minds, then radicalize their discipleship . . . and their changed lives influenced others.

We can do the same. We too are living in a calamitous century, a century which Alexander Solzhenitsyn calls the bloodiest in history. The moral pilings have been ripped from beneath society's piers leaving mankind adrift and modern culture floundering at sea. The absolutes by which we once steered course have been abandoned.

> You shall have no other gods before me.
> You shall not make for yourself a graven image. . . .
> You shall not take the name of the Lord your God in
>   vain. . . .
> Remember the sabbath day, to keep it holy. . . .
> Honor your father and your mother. . . .
> You shall not kill.
> You shall not commit adultery.
> You shall not steal.
> You shall not bear false witness against your neighbor.
> You shall not covet. . . .

These are the moorings we must begin to sink again into the sandy shores; it is the decalogue which Christ summarized succinctly in a law of love, "You shall love the Lord your God with all your heart, and with all your soul, and with all your mind. . . . You shall love your neighbor as yourself. On these two commandments depend all the law and the prophets" (Matthew 22:37–40).

When we turn our hearts back to the absolutes which God established when he began to call out one nation, Israel, unto himself—when we understand how Christ fulfilled rather than abolished these ten moral principles, how he transformed them from legalities into a lifestyle of godly love—then we become small lights burning again on the shores of the world; flames flickering in the gathering darkness; reformers whose tiny, single campfires can leap from place to place; incendiary watchfires which call a blinded society back into the light. "Each soul raising itself," says Elizabeth Leseur, "raises the world."

So it is worth turning our hearts toward reformation of the Lord's Day observance; we are part of that generation who can build again the walls that have been torn down, repair the ruined gates, restore the towers, then step anew into this sanctuary, this holy place in time. "This day is holy to the Lord your God; do not mourn or weep." These were Nehemiah's words after the temple worship was restored, the law had been read, and the reformation under his leadership was well on its way. "Go your way, eat the fat and drink sweet wine and send portions to him for whom nothing is prepared; for this day is holy to our Lord; and do not be grieved, for the joy of the Lord is your strength" (Nehemiah 8:9, 10).

"The Sabbath itself is a sanctuary which we build, a sanctuary in time," writes Rabbi Abraham Heschel in *Meaning for Modern Man* (p. 29). We can restore the Lord's Day in Sabbath celebration; let us mourn not nor weep, but let us get ready with reformers' hearts determined to lift ourselves, to lift our worlds.

GETTING-STARTED
EXERCISES

A Revised Calendar to help you adjust to the weekly rhythm of the sacred.

A Check-off Chart to make sure you recognize Christ's presence in church each Sunday.

Ten Exercises to prepare your heart for Sunday worship.

A "Pre-empted for Spiritual Prime Time" Card to remind yourself and others to avoid distractions which interfere with Sunday preparation.

A REVISED CALENDAR TO HELP YOU ADJUST
TO THE WEEKLY RHYTHM OF THE SACRED

This calendar on the next page is designed to give you eight weeks of practice in adjusting your lifestyle to the weekly rhythm of the sacred. Eight weeks is fifty-six days in all and is enough time to get you started in a positive modification of your living patterns. The idea behind the calendar is to place Sunday in the middle of the week in order to make it the high point. The three days leading to Sunday are days of anticipation; the three days following Sunday are days of reflection.

Notice that blanks have been placed under each three-day grouping. Attempt to fill in the blanks each week: "I'll make this coming Sunday special for you, Jesus, by ———" and "Jesus, here's what I'll carry in my heart from this last Sunday ———."

If you find this concept to be helpful, the calendar is designed so that you can xerox this page from *Making Sunday Special* to provide further eight-week revised calendars to truly make this way of thinking a discipline in your life.

I'll make this coming Sunday special for you, Jesus, by . . .

Jesus, here's what I'll carry in my heart from this last Sunday . . .

1	2	3	**4**	5	6	7
8	9	10	**11**	12	13	14
15	16	17	**18**	19	20	21
22	23	24	**25**	26	27	28
29	30	31	**32**	33	34	35
36	37	38	**39**	40	41	42
43	44	45	**46**	47	48	49
50	51	52	**53**	54	55	56

THURSDAY   FRIDAY   SATURDAY   SUNDAY   MONDAY   TUESDAY   WEDNESDAY

PREPARING YOUR HEART FOR SUNDAY

These Saturday exercises are designed to begin the worshiping process in your heart so that you don't walk into your Sunday service needing to begin the work of worship "cold." Some churches pick a worship theme for each week, or a pastor may be working through a book of the Bible or a topical study. If you are able to discover ahead of time what these themes will be, integrate them into these activities.

Choose one exercise each week. They take very little time and are surprisingly effective in beginning the worship process in the heart.

Check one box each Saturday to show you have completed the assignment of your choice. Ten assignments are provided from which to choose.

EXERCISES

☐ Write a short letter to God, as you might write to a friend. Express how, as you walk with God, you see that he is characterized by a certain attribute. In essence, this will be a written prayer. When you finish the letter, read it aloud to God.

☐ Set aside fifteen minutes on Saturday for a time of private adoration. Think about God. If you are praising him as all powerful, you may see him seated on a throne. If you are praising him for his love, you might imagine Christ on the cross. Then choose a posture appropriate for this mental picture: sitting, kneeling, walking together, etc. Once you have done this, tell Christ how pleased you are that he is characterized by the worship theme of that given Sunday.

☐ Choose a song that expresses your praise to God regarding worship. Through meditation, allow this music to capture your heart today.

☐ Think about God's work in your life. What has God proven himself to be for you? Now share your thoughts with someone else. Complete this exercise by thanking the Lord for the privilege of telling another of his worth.

☐ Look for a passage of Scripture that underscores a worship theme. You might want to choose verses from several parts of the Bible, much like you would if you were preparing a responsive reading. Tell God, "These verses are FROM you, but I also read them TO you." Then read them out loud to the Lord. You might do this as a prayer for your Saturday evening meal.

☐ The Psalmist often affirms God by reviewing how He worked in the past. Spend time looking back on your life. How has the Lord already proven himself to you? Write down on a sheet of paper at least five personal incidents that convince you he is worthy of your praise tomorrow.

☐ Spend fifteen minutes talking with a friend or family member about the Lord. Welcome Christ into your conversation as you remember his promise to be present when even two or three have gotten together in his name. Discuss together how Christ has proven himself in your lives.

☐ Poetry has often been used by God's people to express their adoration and praise. If you are gifted in this way, write something original. If not, find a poem that reflects a worship theme. Take the poem with you to church to silently read to the Lord in the quiet before the service.

☐ Adoration can sometimes be shown through gifts given to the Lord or to someone else on his behalf. In such a case one's prayer is: "Lord, this special gift is given as a way of expressing my praise to you. Accept it, I pray, as from the heart of one who loves you. Amen."

☐ Come up with an original way to express praise to God as you prepare yourself for church tomorrow.

MAKING SURE YOU RECOGNIZE CHRIST'S PRESENCE IN CHURCH EACH SUNDAY

This is a check-off chart to help you get ready for Sunday. These ideas are only suggestions. As you move more and more into developing your own style of preparation, you may want to make up your own check-off chart. Divided into three sections—During the Week, On Saturday, and On Sunday—this page is designed to help you recognize Christ's presence in church.

David often calls the church office during the latter part of the week to check on the sermon topic or to inquire as to hymn selections for Sunday. Most ministers are thrilled to know their parishioners are preparing themselves in this fashion and would be happy to give you such information. Church secretaries who type the bulletin might also be able to let you know when these items are chosen.

Scripture readings in liturgical churches are determined by a lectionary which is often available to parishioners in printed form. By using the lectionary, you can read the scriptures appointed for a particular Sunday ahead of time and prepare your heart to recognize Christ in the Sunday worship service.

MAKING SURE YOU RECOGNIZE
CHRIST'S PRESENCE IN CHURCH
EACH SUNDAY

(Some Suggested Ideas to Help You Get Ready)

	Week	1	2	3	4	5	6	7	8
DURING THE WEEK									
I have mentally determined that Sunday morning with Christ in his church will be the high point of my week.									
I have learned what the main text of the sermon will be and have meditated on that passage.									
I have prepared myself to sing God's praises by reading through the hymns chosen for the service.									
I have carefully considered the offering I want to present to the Lord with gladness.									
I have prayed about inviting a friend who would benefit from being with me in Christ's presence.									
ON SATURDAY									
I have asked Christ to make me sensitive tomorrow to the needs of people in the body who are hurting.									
I have solved the "Sunday clothes hassle" by making sure that what I will wear is ready today.									
I have spent time in confession so all will be right between myself and my Lord when we meet tomorrow.									
I have determined to get to bed early so I will be refreshed and ready for church tomorrow.									
I have planned on sustaining the delight of this time with Christ and his people by guarding against Sunday afternoon infringements.									
ON SUNDAY									
I have gotten up in plenty of time so I will not feel rushed.									
I have programmed my morning so I will not just arrive at church on time, but get there early.									
I have eaten a good breakfast, so an empty stomach will not detract from my worship.									
I have my Bible in hand plus a pen and paper for taking notes.									
I have left for church with a great sense of expectancy because I know Christ will be there.									

PRE-EMPTED FOR SPIRITUAL PRIME TIME

The idea here is to make a card to put on the knob of your television set, or one to slip into a book as a place marker, in order to remind yourself and those with whom you live that Sunday is spiritual prime time and that you want to remove those influences which might distract your attention from being focused on Christ, on prayer, on making Sunday the spiritually nourishing day it was intended to be. Create your own card or make a copy of this one and cut out the shaded area.

We also slip this card on doorknobs when privacy for prayer is desired, thereby notifying folks that a section of time without interruptions is needed.

Pre-empted for Spiritual

Prime Time

9

The Sacred Rhythm of Work and Play

WHEN AN INTENSE YOUNG MAN with reformer inclinations marries a free-spirited young woman who equates *work* with "to be coerced," there is bound to be a clash. His dedication takes a briefcase even to extended family gatherings, a symptom of a true workaholic. On the other hand, her woman-of-leisure mentality pictures literary discussions at breakfast (with someone else to wash the dishes), lunch with a friend after viewing the latest art institute exhibit (while a nanny watches the children), and evenings set aside for reading (with a cook to prepare dinner).

I hate anything which causes me to sweat; while for David, work is his play. We have had much with which to come to terms on this issue. Our marriage has become a laboratory in which to synthesize a theology of work and a theology of leisure. Surprisingly, the whole concept of the rhythm of the sacred has freed both of us to be what

God intended us to be in the process of learning to observe Sunday with a Sabbath heart. Our tension between work and play is being resolved by an enlightened understanding of the spiritual principle of *recreation* which renews our physical, emotional, and psychological being.

To some Christians, work represents the *summum bonum*—man's highest good. They feel guilty if they take time out for themselves, if they spend money on vacations, or if they are simply caught napping. (And often they are the backbone of a pastor's stable of volunteer layworkers.)

For other Christians, work is only a financial means to an end—ski excursions, fishing trips, or membership in the racquet ball club. These are the folks who endure their jobs, but can hardly wait for leisurely weekends or evenings of television viewing. A pastor friend in a temperate climate put it this way: "It's hard to get people to work; everyone seems to be out on the tennis courts."

To live for work or pleasure is a form of idolatry that many of us unconsciously practice. And the pursuit of either as an end in itself is fruitless. For the Christian to attempt to recreate outside the context of his relationship with God is to eliminate the most important recreational factor. The gentle cycle of anticipation, participation, and reflection is a divinely established pattern that ensures renewal.

Exodus 20:11 states: "For in six days the Lord made heaven and earth, the sea, and all that is in them, and rested the seventh day; therefore the Lord blessed the sabbath day and hallowed it." This is a model for mankind, not a legalistic code derived by an obdurate deity. The Sabbath-keeping commandment is a gift of mercy from the heart of a loving God who knows the burden, the entrapment, the bitter bondage of work. Studs Terkel in his best-selling book *Working* interviews scores of men and women from a wide variety of occupations and writes: "This book, being about work, is, by its very nature, about violence—to the spirit as well as to the body."

God in love gives us rest; and because he was well-experienced with the wandering heart of his creation, man, he made it into a law. In *You Shall Be As Gods* (1966, p. 195) Erich Fromm writes: "Rest in the sense of the traditional Sabbath concept is quite different from 'rest' being defined as not working, or not making an effort. . . . On the Sabbath, man ceases completely . . . to fight for survival and to sustain his biological life. On the Sabbath, man is fully man, with no task other than to be human."

By resting on the seventh day, God who Himself required no rest, took into consideration man's deepest needs. By this act the divine accommodated the human. Like the adult who bends his knees and squats in order to hold conversation with a child, to be able to engage the child's eyes on a common level, God bends toward man in order to guarantee laughter and love without intimidation.

The purpose of Sabbath rest is physical and emotional renewal, but it is also fellowship—a delightful space on the weekly calendar reserved for becoming better acquainted with ourselves, others, and God; it is a time for good talk, holy laughter, serious ideas, and shared intimacies between Creator and creature. Our souls are replenished, quieted, nurtured, caressed. Rest without spiritual rest is incomplete. One of the reasons for the frantic search for leisure activities in our culture (the rushing off to one weekend event or another, then breathlessly returning when Sunday is ended) is that we cannot find true renewal when we deny the spiritual. The very act of recognizing Christ's presence is a means by which God, from whom mankind has been separated by sin, is now mediated to his people. Emmanuel is one of the names for this divine Son, and it means *God with us*. When we recognize Christ, spiritual restoration occurs; we are linked again to God. The practice of coming home to him each week with the gift of time and full attentiveness restores us in the deepest sense that completes mere physical rest and finally renews us as full people—body, mind, and spirit.

The regulation against unceasing work cannot be completely understood apart from the fact that the Ten Commandments are the laws of a Divine Lover, jealous over the loved one, who declares his own ownership prerogatives. "You shall have no other gods before me" is akin to a fiancée saying, "From now on, you won't date other men, will you?"

When I was dating, my father carefully helped me analyze the strengths and weaknesses of all the young men who came into my life. By inviting me to participate in the process, he developed in me some of the acute psychological canniness he himself possessed. There were only one or two young men of whom Dad truly disapproved, and when he felt I was becoming too emotionally involved, he would set off the early-warning alarm, a no-holds-barred evaluation session. But Dad regarded David with true esteem. He was one suitor in whom could be found few flaws.

One caution Dad did give me, however, after an early evaluation session regarding David, was that he might have a tendency to be somewhat jealous. This proved true early in marriage when David insisted that I burn all my letters from other male friends, which I did. Though surprised at first, I soon began to understand the importance of such marital territorial rights.

When David asked me to burn my letters, it was the same as saying, "I don't want you to keep any reminders of former romantic attachments—no pictures of other loves; no keepsakes; no withered corsages; no physical memories of dates, concerts, and places you have gone with other suitors." God also asks us to put away reminders of other loves—things that divert our attention from him. "You shall not make for yourself a graven image." Whatever occupies your mind most is what you are in danger of adoring—jobs, positions of status, people, our homes, even our ministries. I have often heard the words, "It became a god to me." We must be wary of the contemporary images that tend to obsess our thoughts and set themselves up in the temple God has reserved for himself alone.

I once made David promise not to tell wife jokes, those rib-ticklers that creep into many minister's stock of audience pleasers, but which in the long run subtly degrade the opposite sex, the married relationship, and the whole role of wives everywhere. I wanted him to develop the habit of speaking highly of me just as I would attempt to speak highly of him. God asks the same, "You shall not take the name of the Lord your God in vain."

These laws are laws between the Divine Lover and his beloved. And the fourth commandment ("Remember the sabbath day, to keep it holy. Six days you shall labor, and do all your work; but the seventh day is a sabbath to the Lord your God") is an invitation to mutual belonging—mankind with God, and God with mankind.

One young woman told me she had complained to her new husband about his relatives. His response to her was that she had married him knowing they were his relatives and she would be a lot happier if she just accepted them, which is what she decided she would do. My mother used to say, "When you marry the man; you marry the clan." The six remaining commandments are also laws a Divine Lover gives to his beloved. They are rather in the vein of "Love me; love my family." Honor your father and your mother; you shall not kill; you shall not commit adultery; you shall not steal; you shall not bear false witness; you shall not covet.

And the law of the Sabbath is like an arch that joins these two covenants of love—love God and love your

118 THE HIGH POINT OF THE WEEK

neighbor—and when we understand the Sabbath commandment in its proper context as a law of love, it deeply enriches our regard for God and our regard for our neighbor.

Obdurate legality always kills the spirit of the law of love. In the New Testament, we read of how, at the time of Christ, the rabbinical Sabbath requirements to refrain from work weighed heavily upon the people. Traditionally, according to the observant Jew, there are thirty-nine forbidden acts: ploughing, sowing, reaping, sheaf-making, threshing, winnowing, selecting, sifting, grinding, kneading, etc. But to these, man's pharisaical mind had devised intricate accumulations of restrictions. The prohibition against reaping came to include the prohibition against severing any natural growing plant from its place of growth; accordingly, picking flowers, breaking tree branches, plucking up grass all came to be forbidden. It was against these accumulations of restrictions that Christ who proclaimed himself Lord (or Ruler) of the Sabbath inveighed.

Sabbath, properly understood, is rest from the bondage of work. God, ever a Liberator God, is concerned about our freedom. Psalm 127:2 declares: "It is senseless for you to work so hard from early morning until late at night fearing you will starve to death; for God wants his loved ones to get their proper rest" (TLB). God gives us fifty-two Sabbaths, or seven and a half weeks, of vacation time a year!—time during which we are to do no work. As Thomas Aquinas put it, each week one goes on *ad vacandum divinis*—a day of vacation with God.

Rest is different for all people. I renew by reading, taking walks, listening to music, gardening, having a small group of people in my home, good talks, writing in my journal, prayer. David rests by having time to strategize a future project, driving in the car, sitting down in a theater and watching Shakespeare, roughhousing with our boys, working in his prayer journal.

The Hebrew verb *Shâbath* from which the word *Sabbath* comes, means "to stop, to desist, to cease from doing." This may sound easy, but for some it's difficult to leave anything incomplete. Yet, in one sense, much of our work is always incomplete. A mother always has a new pile of laundry the day after washday; for my husband, there is always another broadcast. Work is only finished temporarily; the fields must be planted each spring, then cultivated, then harvested, then planted again. The condition of the ceaselessness of work is inherent to fallen man—"In the sweat of your face you shall eat bread til you return to the ground . . ." (Genesis 3:19). The secret to this dilemma is to learn to rest on the Sabbath as though all the work were done. Dietrich Bonhoeffer says, "Rest even from the thought of labor."

Isaac Grunfeld defines the *melakhah* (the work) the Jew abstains from on the Sabbath as any "act that shows man's mastery over the world by the constructive exercise of his intelligence and skill." This too can be taken to extremes, but perhaps within gentle boundaries it can also be a helpful rule of thumb. Within the Christian framework, renunciation or the giving up of something is always for the purpose of achieving something else. The *Jewish Catalog* explains this well: "To help us achieve this state of *menuhah* (rest), tradition forbids us to engage in many of our everyday activities. Refraining from these activities frees us for other activities, and a day of rest can then say to us: You can slow your life down. You can have the time to rediscover your family and friends. You can take a long walk, sing songs, dance, make love, have a feast, take a long time to pray, meditate, study, etc. You can talk, smile, laugh, s-l-o-w-l-y—with intense care and joy. A *yom menuhah* frees us in the most basic sense of that word—to rediscover places inside ourselves that can get rusty without use."

I often slip into life cycles of not sleeping well at night. An early riser, I'm fatigued by nine o'clock in the evening. I retire early, sleep lightly, am roused by household noises—the dog barking, children returning home from activities, conversation, doors banging. And as a result, I am often awake for several hours in the middle of the night. These periods usually occur when my mind is overloaded with projects and somehow the whole of myself just can't seem to wind down. How wonderful it is in the middle on one of these cycles to sleep, to sleep deeply, to wake rested, truly renewed. "Oh, I slept well last night!" I will announce to my husband whose sleepless nights within the last years can be counted on one hand.

Sabbath rest is like a good sleep after insomnia. It brings respite in man's cruel struggle for existence, it speaks *shalom* to our restless souls. I am often amazed by just how completely relaxed I become through Sunday observance when in the afternoon I honor the Burton family tradition by napping. (One of the regular activities that took place in my busy, childhood home on Sunday was afternoon naps.) These Sunday afternoon naps are usually a deep sleep, a sign that I have allowed the creative initiative so integral to my personality to become still. Rabbi Abraham Heschel, in *The Sabbath: Its Meaning for Modern Man*, defines this *menuhah* as "happiness and stillness, as peace and harmony." And that is often what I experience, with or without the traditional nap. Observing Sunday with Sabbath understanding is like waking and thinking gratefully, *Oh I have slept well.*

Our family is attempting to celebrate the weekly festival which honors the presence of the Messiah/Lord of the Sabbath who now inhabits his people, the church. Through this attempt David and I are experiencing a reconciliation in the work/play division in our marriage.

For David, developing a Sabbath heart has meant learning to recreate. When we observe Sunday, the day of Christ's resurrection, with Sabbath understanding, a resurrection process goes on in each of us. Physical and spiritual renewal are programmed into the computer of the workaholic mentality. One "dies" to the demands and clamor, to the grand dreams of human productivity, and "rises" to a new life of rest in God.

It is interesting to note that Christ's last words on the cross were, "It is finished." With this utterance the veil of the temple was rent in two, signifying that the barrier between God and man was removed in the reconciling act of Christ. We then become his "new creation." "Therefore, if any one is in Christ, he is a new creation; the old has passed away, behold the new has come" (2 Corinthians 5:17).

When we cease from our work and let Christ do his work within us, we realize that our work is not so important. We can stop and the world goes on. It is God's activity that is important, not ours. It is finally the death and resurrection of Christ that allowed fellowship with God to be a perpetual covenant. When we participate in his resurrected life by the memorial of Sunday, when we bring to that memorial day a Sabbath understanding, "We should," as Jonathan Edwards says, "have sympathy with Christ in His joy. He was refreshed on this day; we should be refreshed as those whose hearts are united with His."

Conversely, I know that one must joyfully participate in Sunday without the nagging reminder of unmet deadlines and unfinished housework. I have six days in which to complete as much as can be completed, and then I can truly put aside the weight of responsibilities. By starting early to anticipate Sunday, I find that I am better organized in my housework, my writing, and my broadcasting schedule; I even consider how many personal relationships I can include during the week—all with the wonderful realization that on Saturday, I will begin to rest, to rest deeply, to put aside these obligations and simply be.

The dread of the coercion of work has disappeared because the restful rhythm of the sacred spills into Monday and Tuesday. I use Sunday to vault me into the next week! I use Sunday, this special time, to keep me disciplined for the other days.

> That which is set apart from other things as "holy" is so distinguished only in order that it may imbue with holiness and consecration also every phase of life taking place beyond its confines. In the same manner, the Seventh Day was set apart from the six working days only so that its Sabbath spirit might permeate all of weekday life.
>
> —*Hirsch Siddur*

I am learning that all days are holy, but some are more so. Work finished allows me to devote full attention to enjoying the Lord's presence.

Scripture is filled with rituals of God-ordained festivals, feasts, and celebrations. Some are nationalistic holidays, others are more religious in their significance—but all are periods set aside for joyful participation. The Christian tradition, too, has sought to mark holy days, such as Christmas and Easter, and to participate in them with joy and worship.

The Christ who healed on the Sabbath proclaimed, "My Father is working still, and I am working" (John 5:17). He also said, "The sabbath was made for man, not man for the sabbath" (Mark 2:27). Christ held work and recreation in proper tension. He was a Sabbath-keeper dismayed by the legalities that crushed its celebrative life. His work, the redemption and restoration of the world, did not inhibit his presence at festivals, feasts, and celebrations. And when we, his human creation, his new creations, learn to participate in the sacred rhythm of his design, we take his presence into all of life, leaving behind (as David and I have) the extremes of the Protestant work ethic and the compulsive leisure ethic.

God's timepiece sanctifies both the work need and the leisure need, preserves individuals alone and in culture and protects us from the aberration of extremes. The Sabbath principle is God's holy design for recreation; it is the gift of a Divine Lover to his beloved to preserve her from the "violence" of work.

As we keep or break the Sabbath day, we nobly save or meanly lose the last and best hope by which man arises.
                                                    —Abraham Lincoln

10

Lord's Day Participation

SOREN KIERKEGAARD tells a parable about two beggars seeking admission to a successful city church. One laments that he has tried to enter for years, but simply doesn't fit in with the sort of folk who worship there. The second beggar comforts him, saying he has been standing in the cold for centuries.

"Sir, tell me your name," says the first.

"Jesus Christ," comes the stark reply.

We need to restore our Lord's Day observance with Sabbath understanding, and we need to participate in the special day itself as though Christ had actually been invited to be a part of the congregation.

How long has it been since you or your family or your friends left church on Sunday morning literally captured by the supernatural truth of having met with the living Christ?

I'm not asking whether church was important to you, or if you liked it, or whether the sermon was profitable for your spiritual growth. What is being asked is: How long has it been since you left church on a Sunday morning conscious that the living Christ had ministered to you? And being convinced of this, were you overwhelmed, deeply moved, startled to the center of your being?

To encounter the living Christ, Sunday after Sunday, is the crux of meaningful Sunday worship, and we have to learn how to welcome Christ to our churches each Lord's Day, we must develop the discipline of a heightened Christ consciousness. Paul writes in his first letter to Timothy, chapter 3:14, 15: "I am writing these instructions to you so that, . . . you may know how one ought to behave in the household of God, which is the church of the living God."

David came home one day with a new Tom-Sawyer-like idea for Sunday worship participation. It was an exercise he called "The Sunday Search," and it proved to be every bit as successful as Tom Sawyer's fence-painting idea. I was skeptical at first, particularly as to our children's willing involvement, but the more we painted the fence in our personal lives, the more the idea grew until it became one of the most meaningful spiritual exercises we practice on Sunday morning.

The idea is to participate in Sunday worship by searching for how Christ will speak *to* and *through* you.

This means we go to church asking first: *How will Christ speak to me this morning?* When we were learning to implement this concept, we reminded the children before we left the house to be aware of ways Christ might speak to them. Now the Sunday Search is a practice so integral to our experience that it has become a natural activity.

Christ can speak to our hearts in a variety of ways. He can speak by his Holy Spirit through Scripture, through the Sunday school lesson, through the sermon. He can be present in the words of hymns, in choir anthems, in musical solos. Christ can move our hearts and minds as we meditate on prayers, or as we hear the call to worship; we can be reminded of him in architecture, stained-glass windows, Communion (a whole topic in itself). There's a silent inner nudge to the conscience, or a direct answer to a question you've been asking, or a strong sense of conviction regarding something awry in your life.

So we need to attend church listening carefully to what is being taught and preached.

Getting to church early enough to read through the hymns ahead of time enhances the possibility of his special word touching our hearts as we sing them without fumbling over matching the lyrics to the notes. Getting to church early enough enables us to quiet our hearts, to pray, to begin to actively remind ourselves in the silence that the Spirit of Christ is truly present, a most wonderful privilege; and if we are attentive, he will make himself known. This is an interlude when we can allow the Holy Spirit to remind us of faults and attitudes we need to confess but somehow overlooked in other private times of confession.

David closes his eyes when Scriptures are read and imagines the human author—Moses or Isaiah, the apostle Paul, or Luke—reading aloud while writing under the inspiration of the Holy Spirit.

Other people can be a means through whom Christ speaks. Has anyone ever caught your arm and said, "I've thought about you this week and I wanted to tell you . . . " and you were warmed with encouragement, comforted, sustained? Perhaps you have been suffering from loneliness and someone said, "Can you join me for lunch today? I would love to get to know you better." That was Christ speaking to you by answering your prayer.

How will Christ speak *to* me?

If you are actively participating in the Sunday Search,

his means of speaking to you can be wondrous! One
Sunday David and I invited some friends who were new
to our community to attend our church. They had two
small children; the younger, a boy, became wiggly during the time of Communion, so David took him on his lap
and did the old rub-the-back-awhile routine. After a bit,
I overheard this little fellow as he turned and sotto voce
said to David, "You weigh more than you should don't
you?"

It was my delight to begin to reinforce this godly communication via the mouth of babes by asking after
church, "Did Christ speak *to* you this morning, David?"

On another Sunday, I was sitting in church praying
during the time of private confession when I heard an
inner voice (almost as loud in my spiritual ears as that of
David's little friend's) say, "You are contributing to the
evil in a certain relationship about which you have so
frequently prayed. You need to confess your part and
repent." I am learning to be glad that Christ speaks in
interior silence and not in the amplified public address
system we so often wish upon him!

Christ is always waiting to speak to our hearts; the
problem is not that he isn't communicative but that we
allow him to remain a beggar standing in the cold without giving him access to our innermost habitations.

I have found that Christ can speak in church in my
mind in remarkable ways. The pastor's sermon triggers
something that relates to another thought that bounces
off memory and snaps the switch that lights a bulb in my
head that shows me the answer to something I'd been
groping around in the dark after!

How will Christ speak to me? is rule number one for
the Sunday Search.

Number two of only three rules is *discovering how
Christ will speak through me*. How can Christ reach out
to someone *through* me?

Again, it's not that the living Christ doesn't want to

minister when the body is gathered; it's just that much of modern Christianity has assumed a consumerism mentality. Churchgoers are out shopping for the best "spiritual bargain." They ask not: "What can I bring to Christ and to his body Sunday after Sunday?" but: "What's in it for *me?* What can *I* get out of it? What's the best buy in return for *my* weekly offering?"

One friend's mother taught her: We don't go to church with empty baskets, but with baskets full. Part of our expectation for the Sunday morning worship experience must be that Christ will manifest his presence in the congregation when we give out of our full baskets to one another.

Interestingly enough, the Sabbath commandment in Deuteronomy 5:12–15 lists quite a few people to whom Sabbath rest is extended ". . . you, or your son, or your daughter, your manservant, or your maidservant, or your . . . cattle, or the sojourner who is within your gates. . . ." It includes family members, workers and hired people, the dumb beasts, as well as guests and strangers; and it grows outward in concentric rings from intimate relationships to those of mere acquaintances. Sabbath was a day for specializing in acts of love and mercy to family, friends, and mere acquaintances. Christ quotes from the Old Testament writers while teaching on true Sabbath understanding, "And if you had known what this means, 'I desire mercy, and not sacrifice,' you would not have condemned the guiltless" (Matthew 12:7).

Mercy, in fact, was the point of the healing which Christ so regularly extended on the Sabbath. He asks, "Is it lawful to heal on the sabbath?" and according to both Mark and Luke, he answers his own question by asking another question of principle. "Is it lawful on the sabbath to do good or to do harm, to save life or to kill?" Here he substitutes the verb *to heal* with the more expansive term *to do good* in order to include all kinds of benevolent activities within the intention of the Sabbath law, making it clear that the original divine intent was that of showing concern and compassion for others.

Sunday, when observed within the Sabbath principle also becomes a mercy day, a day when we look for ways to celebrate the fact that Christ has redeemed us from our sins by finding ways to demonstrate his love to others. Therefore, we need to go to church anticipating how Christ will speak *through* us to others. This is a difficult concept for many people to understand, so let me again illustrate with examples out of my own life.

One of the prayers I pray as I sit in quiet on Sunday morning is: *Who is there you want me to minister to this day?* Often as simple an act as a warmly spoken greeting can give deep welcome to one who is lonely. The right question asked in the right way often elicits grateful response.

David regularly slips an extra fifteen to twenty dollars into his pants pocket. This isn't offering money but money to be used if he is divinely nudged by need. Once a college student, a friend of our son, attended church. "Glad to see you here, Eric," said David. "We've missed you."

"Well, I missed being in church and I got here," said our son's friend. "But I'm not sure I'm going to get home." His gas tank was low, and he had no money to buy more fuel. David immediately gave him the fifteen dollars he had slipped into his pocket that morning, not needing to ask himself, "Should I give him money? How much money should I give him? Will he be embarrassed if I do? What should I say?"—all questions which can debilitate ministering responses.

When we were in a city pastorate and many people struggled financially, we often put a bag of groceries in the car and had it to share when we sensed through careful listening that someone didn't have quite enough resources to make it through the next week.

Listening in itself is a way Christ can speak *through* us to others. People rarely have enough undivided attention. It is healing to feel as though someone has given you a concentrated fifteen minutes of listening time. Catherine de Hueck Doherty writes in *Poustinia: Christian Spirituality of the East for Western Man* that it is possible to listen a person's soul into existence. Then instead of saying, "I'll pray for you," do it! Sit quietly at the front of the auditorium or slip into an empty classroom and pray together. Spontaneous prayer is a powerful and neglected means of Sunday ministry.

Sharing a Sunday meal is another way Christ speaks to others through us. I often prepare a brunch menu and go to church not really sure who will be our guests. My prayer again is: *Lord, who is here to whom you wish me to minister?* David and the children know they are free to invite friends and acquaintances. Our Sunday brunches have often been surprise feasts at which we have celebrated the joy of meeting new personalities.

Calling people whom we haven't seen in church is also a way of reaching out, of saying, "I really missed you, and wanted you to know it." Even phone calls to those who have been in church are beneficial. Often I have a leftover thought, an interrupted discussion, an idea about an item of need which is completed by a simple phone call, bringing satisfactory closure which says, "I haven't forgotten you. I've been thinking more about our conversation."

Writing notes on Sunday evening is a discipline I am attempting to establish. A short letter written to the staff, to the musicians while I am still full of the warmth of Sunday feeling is another simple way by which Christ speaks *through* me to people in our church.

Even little children can be taught to minister Christ; in fact, they are often best of all at it. A spontaneous smile, a hug, the endearing comments only unsophisticated children make can melt the icy soul of the most crotchety adult. One two-year-old in our church greets me with an exuberant, "My friend!" And if she is feeling quite comfortable, I often receive lavish hugs and kisses as well. Believe me, I know Christ has touched me through the embrace of a child. We need to be teaching our children to minister Christ on Sunday morning.

The Sunday Search is a spiritual discipline designed in the form of a game with three rules. We go to church anticipating, *How will Christ speak to me?* (rule one) and *How will Christ speak through me?* (rule two). Then *We must talk about it* (rule three). There must be a time of debriefing. This can be done over the phone with a friend if you are single or if your family is not yet playing the game. This can be done over lunch or on the drive home from church; but the Sunday Search is not complete until you have shared your experience with someone else.

These debriefing sessions with our family are some of the most precious times that we share spiritually with each other. Surprisingly, they are frequently accompanied by laughter and tears. Verbal and emotional closure is brought to our Sabbath/Sunday weekly journey in these discussions. We find that we can reveal the struggle of our human pilgrimages with each other, and that the spiritual unseen world is often made more tangible when we talk about it.

These family discussions become so lively we often find ourselves saying (because we drive two cars to church due to juggling six schedules), "Don't talk about the Sunday Search until we get home. We all want to hear what everyone else has to share!"

Parents often ask how they can introduce their teens to this concept. Or a wife will wonder how she can invite her husband to participate in a way that won't offset him. My reply is always: Begin whitewashing the fence by yourself. Like Tom Sawyer, make sure that the experience is so wonderful to you personally, or to you as a couple, that the rest of the members of your family will want to take the Sunday Search brush in hand.

We don't make people share who are uncomfortable sharing, but generally the experience of talking about Sunday becomes so exciting that those who listen are stimulated by the exchange of ideas and they spontaneously begin to contribute themselves. Believe me, it is hard to stay uninvolved.

One experience from our family life illustrates the whole concept of this Sunday discipline.

David is responsible for a national radio ministry that, like many ministries, experiences cyclical funding crises. We know from year to year, for instance, that our summer donations will be low. During one of these times, he really wondered if we could possibly go on; but we were also so far behind that the other consideration was, if we quit, did we have enough assets to pay off our debt?

These financial burdens can often be excruciating for the men and women who shoulder them in order to do the work God has called them to do.

During the midst of this crisis, one Sunday morning we received an early phone call from a station owner who challenged David's spiritual integrity because of the money owed by our ministry. All David could say was that he agreed with this man's concern and had constantly brought that exact matter to God's attention himself. Nevertheless, he went to church that morning with a giant stress headache that prohibited him from concentrating much on how Christ was speaking *to* him.

David tells how our oldest son, at that time a senior in college, slipped into the church pew and in a little while, without knowing about this recent pressure, placed his arm around his dad and squeezed his far shoulder. Then he kept his hand there during the entire sermon. David testifies to how this warmed and comforted him, "My son had received strength from me for much of his life, but now I was receiving strength from him." When the worship time was ended, David's headache had also disappeared.

We arrived home, in full family force, and while waiting for the finishing touches on the meal, we began to debrief the Sunday Search game. Again, these are tender moments as we allow one another glimpses of the work God is doing in our hearts. When our oldest son shared, he told about how Christ had spoken to him but then said, "I can't really think of a way that Christ spoke through me. I guess this is just one of those Sundays when nothing happened."

There was a moment of quiet and then a father told a son how Christ had used him to minister mightily through loving touch.

Lay people in the pew can alter the overall Sunday morning worship experience by preparing their hearts to experience Christ in his church. We have thousands of letters testifying to this transforming spiritual discipline. One person writes, "I thought something was wrong with my church, but after I began playing the Sunday Search game, I discovered what was wrong was really me."

Sunday worship has become so meaningful that I have a small Sunday notebook set aside for notes on the sermon, for the special communication of Christ to and through me, for thoughts that come to my quieted mind that I don't want to forget. Late Sunday afternoon, I try to bring closure to the whole experience by holding private vespers. I take my notebook, go over that day's notations, then jot down a few prayers of thanksgiving and praise. It is my personal way of saying farewell to what has become the best day of the week for me.

Our youngest son, at fourteen, was a budding artist. He had illustrated several children's books, developed a portfolio, drawn cartoons for the school newspaper, and had sent off his first free-lance submission to a national magazine. Day after day, week after week, his first question after returning home from school was, "Any mail for me?" Being a free-lance writer myself, I well understood his vigil and had warned about the vagaries of free-lance submission. Finally his cartoons were returned with an instructional letter from the art editor—Jeremy's first career rejection.

Jeremy took a long bike ride, and when he came home, I discovered a mature young man instead of a disappointed teen. He said something amazing to me, "At first I was upset, but the more I rode around, the more I had the impression that God was smiling at me. This has happened a couple of other times recently. In gym, I made some dumb mistakes, three right in a row. I was pretty mad at myself, but then it seemed as though God said *Look, if you had made three mistakes in a week, you wouldn't be so hard on yourself. So you made three bad moves in one hour. No big deal.*" Jeremy shrugged his shoulders as in agreement and said, "I still feel like God is smiling at me."

How wonderful! At fourteen, my son was developing the prayer of listening. I was in my thirties before I even knew such a spiritual dialogue with God was possible. Many Christian adults traverse their entire lives and never experience this kind of two-way communication, this inner conversation with the Holy Spirit. I wondered: *How has this come about? Do we have a mystic among us?* Then I realized that this child has been playing the Sunday Search week after week for several years. Why should I be so surprised that he had developed the capacity of spiritual hearing, of inviting Christ into all of life?

The spiritual exercise of the Sunday Search has not only made Sunday special and church-attending a joy for the Mains household, but by increasing our spiritual attentiveness, it has influenced every day of the week.

Truly a miracle unfolds in the church of the living God when Christians learn to experience Christ's presence week after week; but it is a miracle that also has the potential to transform the rest of daily living.

GOING ON THE SUNDAY SEARCH

Use this chart to record your Sunday Search experiences for eight weeks.

SUNDAYS   MY RESPONSE

1. How Christ spoke TO me: _____

How Christ spoke THROUGH me: _____

I TALKED ABOUT these experiences with: _____

2. How Christ spoke TO me: _____

How Christ spoke THROUGH me: _____

I TALKED ABOUT these experiences with: _____

3. How Christ spoke TO me: _____

How Christ spoke THROUGH me: _____

I TALKED ABOUT these experiences with: _____

4. How Christ spoke TO me: _____

How Christ spoke THROUGH me: _____

I TALKED ABOUT these experiences with: _____

5. How Christ spoke TO me: _____

How Christ spoke THROUGH me: _____

I TALKED ABOUT these experiences with: _____

6. How Christ spoke TO me: _____

How Christ spoke THROUGH me: _____

I TALKED ABOUT these experiences with: _____

7. How Christ spoke TO me: _____

How Christ spoke THROUGH me: _____

I TALKED ABOUT these experiences with: _____

8. How Christ spoke TO me: _____

How Christ spoke THROUGH me: _____

I TALKED ABOUT these experiences with: _____

11

Making
Time Holy

THE CONGREGATION that David pastored in the inner city of Chicago during the 1960s and '70s was composed of young adults, many of whom were disillusioned with the traditional churches of their past. They wore hand embroidered jeans, resale shop finds, fur coats twenty-five years old, and because they were artistic, avant-garde, and unabashed, they put the flotsam and jetsam of Salvation Army stores together with originality and creativity. On an average, they were twenty-eight years of age.

Theresa with her white hair was a welcome anomaly. In her seventies, slightly rotund, wearing sensible, sturdy shoes, she was a contrast in style. This former nun, who had left the convent earlier in her life as the result of a spiritual conversion experience, compassionately demonstrated unusual sensitivity to the demands on my life—four small children, pastoring responsibilities, a house full of guests and parishioners, people in trouble living with us, and a need to find expression for my own personal gifts. She volunteered to come once a week and help me clean.

I will never forget rosy-faced Theresa arriving at my door, having taken public transportation across the city, shopping bags in hand, and ready to do whatever needed to be done. She refused payment and wouldn't allow David to pick her up or drive her home. No task was demeaning. She simply found a way to express her love for us by scrubbing and dusting and cooking. I remember this dear woman well, her slight lisp, her soft aging skin. She ministered to me then, and in my memory, she ministers almost as meaningfully to me now.

Theresa even had a retroactive influence on my prayer life. She had learned to pray in the convent. She had a clock in her home that chimed on the quarter hour, and she used it to remind her to continue in the work of praying without ceasing. Now whenever my antique gingerbread mantle clock marks the hour and the half hour, I frequently remember Theresa. To mark the hours, the half-hours, the quarter-hours with prayer is one of my personal spiritual goals (which I expect I will only be able to do when I am old and approaching infirmity).

Mankind has measured time by the sun, by dripping water, by falling grains of sand—any number of ways. But the first steps toward the mechanical measurement of time began in religious communities which were anxious to perform promptly and regularly their duties to God. Monks needed to know the times for appointed prayers. And these first mechanical devices were designed not to show time but to sound time, the earliest being small monastic alarms which woke the *custos horologii*, the guardian of the clock who would then go and strike a large bell, usually set in a tower, so that all could hear.

These monastic clocks marked the canonical hours, times of days proscribed by church canons, rules for devotion. After the sixth century, and due to the influence of Benedict, the canonical hours were standardized at seven. Distinct prayers were specified for these times: matins and nocturns at midnight; lauds, following immediately after; prime at sunrise; terce at midmorning; sext at noon; nones at midafternoon; vespers and evening prayer at eventide; and compline at bedtime.

According to Daniel Boorstin in his book *The Discoverers:* "The broadcasting medium of the medieval town was bells. Since the human voice could not reach all who needed to hear a civic announcement, bells told the hours, summoned help to extinguish a fire, warned of an approaching enemy, called men to arms, brought them to work, sent them to bed, knelled public mourning at the death of a king, sounded public rejoicing at the birth of a prince or a coronation, celebrated the election of a pope or a victory in war."

An inscription on one bell boasted, "I mourn death, I disperse the lightning, I announce the Sabbath, I rouse the lazy, I scatter the winds, I appease the bloodthirsty." In Latin it read: *Funera plango, fulmina frango, Sabbath pango, excito lentos, dissipo ventos, paco cruentos.*

While traveling in the Middle East, I was often wakened by the Muslim early morning call to prayer, a wail from the nearby mosque. The devout Muslim stops what he is doing, unrolls his prayer rug, and genuflects with his forehead to the ground seven times a day. In Israel of old there was a daily morning and evening sacrifice and the Jew prayed at the three appointed times during the day, the third, sixth, and ninth hours. In Acts 3:1, we are told that Peter and John went up into the temple at "the hour of prayer, the ninth hour," and in Acts 10:9, we read that Peter went up on the housetop to pray at "about the sixth hour."

And those of us in modern Christendom feel smug

when we have a quiet time once a week, and we are hardly appalled when we read that the professional minister averages only about seven minutes in prayer per day. The average church-going Western Christian has lost something very important—a concept of the holiness of time.

One reason for this loss is that we are not marking the time of Sunday with Sabbath understanding. Sabbath is not a place we go to perform rituals, but a time set aside to be with God, ourselves, and others. Being nonmaterial, but set in time, the Sabbath, unlike temple sacrifice, is an incorruptible monument of God's covenant with man. Earthquakes cannot shake it, fire cannot sear it, war cannot destroy it.

Observing Sunday with Sabbath understanding makes prayer through the rest of the week more possible; it marks one day as being holier than the others, enabling us consequently, to sanctify the other moments of weekly time. Here in this sanctuary in time, we are reminded that the spiritual other world in reality exists. Prepared for it, we can step into it.

We modern Christians live in a secular culture, a society which rejects the supernatural good; and tragically, we ourselves have become so acculturized we have no idea what the sacred really is, how God intended it to coinhere with material life, or what we have lost. *We are gravely in danger of becoming a secularized church.* And we have no business pointing our fingers at a godless, corrupted world if we, first of all, do not press them against our own hearts which hold such feeble comprehensions of the holy. Oh, we know all there is to know about holy legalisms; we comprehend the "thou shall nots." But we have blurred, faded, spotty, glaucoma-clouded vision when it comes to holy actualities; we do not know how to live out the relationship of a holy divine romance.

The test of our own secularization is how we view and

how we use time. Too often ours is a selfish view . . . It is *our* time, to do with as *we* please, either lived out accidentally or compulsively with few weekly memorials, fewer still daily altars, next-to-no hourly markers which say, "This time is really God's—this day, this hour, these minutes. I will bow my head to my rug and bend to him."

I am learning that when I pray, I desecularize myself, that part of me that's "prone to wander, . . . prone to leave the God I love." When I pause in my time— weekly, daily, hourly—I put one foot into his time and stride this great divide between the human and the divine, and the more I straddle this chasm in my personal universe, the closer the holy comes. I am frequently not only aware of God, but flushed full of him. Time which used to crack only slightly to make place for him, now folds outward, and he seeps into, invades wholly, engulfs completely the rest of the moments of my life, taking gentle advantage of the rare keyhole windows in the spaces in my soul.

He is an importunate lover, demanding concentration. I am at the point in my spiritual appointments with him that when I leave these allotted moments, he uses them and haunts my soul with love thoughts the rest of my day.

Not only do we desecularize ourselves when we give God time (weekly, daily, and hourly), we desecularize our environments—home, church, personal worlds. A peculiar people, together desecularizing themselves, desecularize villages, communities, nations. We diligently, faithfully, day-in and day-out bring the firm, unseen spiritual into the seen infirmity of living. That is the little understood work of the Christian. He plants the spiritual in life.

In an article titled "The Man Who Planted Trees and Grew Happiness" published in *Friends of Nature,* Jean Giono tells the story of Elzeard Bouffier, a shepherd he met in 1913 in mountain heights unknown to tourists in a region of the Alps thrusting down into Provence, France. At this time the area was a barren and colorless land where nothing grew but wild lavender. Former villages were now desolate, springs had run dry, and over this high unsheltered land, the wind blew with unendurable ferocity.

While mountain climbing, Giono began searching for water and came to a shepherd's hut into which he was invited for a meal and to spend the night. Giono tells of his host's evening activity after the simple dinner.

> The shepherd went to fetch a small sack and poured out a heap of acorns on the table. He began to inspect them, one by one, with great concentration, separating the good from the bad. . . . When he had set aside a large enough pile of good acorns he counted them out by tens, meanwhile eliminating the small ones or those which were slightly cracked, for now he examined them more closely. When he had thus selected one hundred perfect acorns he stopped and he went to bed.

Giono discovered that the shepherd had been planting trees on the wild hillsides. In three years he had planted 100,000 of which 20,000 had sprouted. Of the 20,000, the quiet man expected to lose half to rodents or to the caprice of nature. There remained 10,000 oak trees to grow where nothing had grown before.

At that time in his life, Elzeard Bouffier was fifty-five years of age. Giono informed him that in thirty years his 10,000 oaks would be magnificent. The shepherd answered simply that if God granted him life, in thirty years he would have planted so many more that the 10,000 would be insignificant.

Returning to the mountainside after the First World War, Giono discovered a veritable forest and a chain-reaction in creation. The desolation was giving way to verdant growth, water flowed in the once empty brooks.

The wind scattered seeds, and the ecology, sheltered by a leafy roof and bonded to the earth by a mat of spreading roots, became hospitable. Willows, rushes, meadows, gardens, flowers were birthed. The once desolate villages were rehabited.

Officials came to admire this reforestation. A *natural* forest, they exclaimed, had sprung up spontaneously, none suspecting the precision and dedication of so exceptional a personality as the tree-planter who worked in total solitude, without need for human acclaim. Giono shared his knowledge of Bouffier's work with one forestry officer, "a man who knew how to keep silent."

Commenting on Bouffier's health at age seventy-five, Giono writes: "In the direction from which we had come the slopes were covered with trees twenty to twenty-five feet tall. I remembered how the land had looked in 1913: a desert. . . . Peaceful, regular toil; the vigorous mountain air; frugality and, above all, serenity in the spirit had endowed this old man with awe-inspiring health. He was one of God's athletes. I wondered how many more acres he was going to cover with trees."

Giono returned again to the region after World War II. Thirty kilometers away from the lines, the shepherd had peacefully continued his work, ignoring the war of 1939 as he had ignored that of 1914. The reformation of land had continued. The once near-savage conditions had continued to give way to "Lazarus out of the tombs." Eight years later the whole countryside glowed with health and prosperity.

On the site of the ruins I had seen in 1913 now stand neat farms. . . . The old streams, fed by the rains and snows that the forest conserves, are flowing again. . . . Little by little the villages have been rebuilt. People from the plains, where land is costly, have settled here, bringing youth, motion, the spirit of adventure. Along the roads you meet hearty men and women, boys and

girls who understand laughter and have recovered a taste
for picnics. Counting the former population, unrecog-
nizable now that they live in comfort, more than 10,000
people owe their happiness to Elzeard Bouffier.

This illustration moves me, stirs me deeply because I
believe this is an example of the work of holy people
who, unacclaimed and unknown nevertheless quietly,
without adulation, go about persistently digging holes
into the stripped and striated, spiritually barren world,
planting firm, round acorns, seedlings, and saplings;
100,000 at first, 10,000 of which take root and survive.
And the holy ones go on planting, planting, planting
until spiritual ecology is restored—until the sacred
blooms, takes hold, spreads, leafs, shelters.

Each time I pray, I plant; each morning office of
prayer I observe, each compline, each hour given to
intercession, each quieted journey of praise as I walk
three-and-a-half miles for exercise, each moment of listening to him, each recorded word in a prayer journal is
a planting session. I join hands with other intercessors,
old men and women whose names I do not know, but
who are present with me in this spiritual network,
planting trees in the wilderness of our world, planting
weekly, daily, hourly, each time clocks chime the
quarter-hour, the half, the full-hour; *matins, nocturns,
lauds, prime, terce, sext, nones, vespers, compline.*

All this to testify, that whereas I have kept a prayer
notebook for nearing two decades, it was only after we
began to set aside one day a week as holy unto the Lord,
that the discipline of daily regular prayer (not every
hour, but often hourly) began to take firm, insistent,
rapid, importunate place in my spiritual life.

All days are holy, but some are more so; all moments
can be sacred but not unless we set some aside to be
intensely so.

Nature is always an excellent illustrator of spiritual

principles. For example, the jungle is being deforested along the Amazon River Basin in Brazil. A study, headed by Eneas Salati of the University of Sao Paulo in Brazil, shows that forested land returns ten times the moisture to the atmosphere as deforested land and produces 50 percent of the rain that falls on it. The research "gives very strong evidence that cutting down tropical rain forests reduces rainfall and increases temperature." Although Salati's study confines itself to climate regulation in the area of tropical forests, experts believe that the findings also have implications for global weather patterns.

Our world, the spiritual world which we must hold dear, is being defoliated, deforested. We have become a dehydrated people, with meager supernatural life, dwelling in desert places of the soul. God meant what he said, "Remember the sabbath day, to keep it holy. Six days you shall labor, and do all your work; but the seventh day is a sabbath to the Lord your God . . . for in six days the Lord made heaven and earth, the sea, and all that is in them, and rested the seventh day; therefore the Lord blessed the sabbath day and hallowed it" (Exodus 20:8–11).

We don't keep nine commandments but capriciously chop down one because it inconveniences us. Ezekiel complains, "You have despised my holy things, and profaned my sabbaths" (22:8). There is a hunger in our society for the forests, the leafy sanctuaries, the shaded paths. In *Turning East,* Harvey Cox maintains that thousands of Westerners are today turning to Eastern meditation because "it provides a modern equivalent of what the observance of Sabbath once did but does no more." But why turn to Eastern meditation with its often unrealistic escape from the sad realities of life? We need a renewal of holiness, a replanting of things sacred.

Christianity's view of the supernatural has always been a real spiritual world coexisting in the midst of material realities. Observing Sunday with Sabbath understanding provides a one-day-a-week interlude in order to catch a glimpse of the divine idea of order, purity, and love. With such a renewed vision, the believer is equipped to live in the present world fully, while looking toward a world to come, living in the now while preparing for eternity.

When Christ came to earth, he also left it without leaving material traces of himself. He left no home he had owned, no belongings he could call his own, no books he had written, no possessions to be inherited by friends, no images painted on papyrus, only an empty tomb and even the location of that is in dispute. Why? For the same reason that God established the memorial of Sabbath in time—because of humankind's tendency to object worship.

Christ left no "thing" of his own which followers could venerate, only the perpetual promise of his spiritual presence, "Lo, I am with you always, to the close of the age" (Matthew 28:20). This reality requires spiritual communion, spiritual knowing, spiritual acquaintance.

We do not experience his spiritual presence because we are not a spiritual people. The barrenness on the hillsides of our souls is caused by a deforestation of the trees that once rooted us to spiritual realities. There is a tree of life we can plant that rapidly grows. Casting shade and capturing rainfall, it provides shelter for more life beneath its branches. That tree is learning to make Sunday special. The understanding of the holiness of time, the understanding of the work/leisure dichotomy, the understanding of spiritual realities, and the consequent understanding of the sacredness of life in its totality—all root deeply in the hospitable soil beneath its spreading boughs. This is a spiritual ecology we can no longer afford to ignore.

PART II

THE
HEART
OF A
SABBATH
KEEPER

Why Love Makes Sunday Special

12

The Gentleman Caller

MANY LIFEFORMS INVISIBLE to the human eye can be discovered when a simple drop of water is viewed through a microscope. The same is true of spiritual truth; that which is too familiar often needs to be examined through another lens. The holy, awesome implications of Sunday have been lost to most contemporary Christians, and this is because one motif from Scripture has fallen into neglect. Our experiential understanding of God's motif, the progressive theme of divine love, is like the broken walls of Jerusalem that Nehemiah returned from exile to restore. We need a reformation in our understanding in order to truly restore Sunday observance with a Sabbath heart.

Without a clear comprehension of how keeping the Sabbath holy fits into this love scheme, law-keeping becomes the justification for obedience with a degeneration into legalism following close behind. Such has been the history of man's attempts to keep God's designs, a perpetual swing of motion from restrictive law to reactionary liberalism.

One lens which often stimulates a fresh view of Scripture for me is the refractive mirror of literature. The words and themes and tales of humanity's common experience often illustrate God's history with man, but they are also illuminated by absolute truth, often beyond what the secular author intended. These discoveries give me great pleasure and aid me in communicating God's truths to myself as well as to others for whom those dramatic holy concepts have lost their meaning.

God's love motif not only saturates holy writ; it is the unspoken longing that lurks in man's literature surprising those of us who seek to find it and casting light on wondrous revelations which should never have grown dim. Perhaps a few glimpses through this lens will help us to set Sabbath/Sunday celebration into its full and impelling context.

For instance, last summer, David and I saw *The Glass Menagerie,* a play written by Tennessee Williams, and ever since, one of the characters has haunted me. The main characters are the Wingfields, a mother Amanda who clings frantically to a lost time; the daughter Laura, a crippled young woman of frail beauty who has failed to establish contact with reality and identifies deeply with her fragile collection of miniature glass animals; the son Tom upon whose restless shoulders the burden of these two dependents weighs heavily.

The character who has haunted me, however, the one about whom I have thought much, is the gentleman caller ("a symbol," says Tom, "of the long delayed, but always expected something that we live for"). Amanda, her voice from the stage languid with accents of the deep South, introduces him first as a symbol from her own past.

One Sunday afternoon in Blue Mountain—your mother received—seventeen!—gentlemen callers! . . . My callers were gentlemen—all! Among my callers were some of the most prominent young planters of the Mississippi Delta—planters and sons of planters! . . . There were the Cutrere brothers, Wesley and Bates. Bates was one of my bright particular beaux . . . and there was that boy that every girl in the Delta had set her cap for! That beautiful, brilliant young Fitzhugh boy from Greene County!

The crucible of this drama, of course, is heated by the insistence of the mother that her son, Tom, should bring home some work acquaintance to be a gentleman caller for the painfully shy and withdrawn Laura.

The last part of the play deals with the coming of a real gentleman caller, a truly nice young man, Jim O'Connor who is unaware of Laura and who, unbeknown to both Tom and Amanda, is engaged to another young woman. But before this fact is revealed, there is a scene of exquisite tenderness where, after a lavishly prepared dinner which stretches the family's already meager means, Jim kindly focuses his attention on Laura. Alone in the living room while the other two are doing dishes, he sees in her a particular uniqueness and lightheartedly asks her to dance to the music floating up the narrow alley from the Paradise Dance Hall, across the murky canyons of tangled clotheslines, garbage cans, and crisscross fire escapes.

Laura protests. She is encumbered by a brace, with one foot shorter than the other, but the young man literally sweeps her around the room for a brief happy moment; they bump into a table, and the unicorn, favored by the young woman, different from the other glass horses, falls to the floor and breaks. Jim apologizes. Then in gentlemanly consideration he recognizes Laura's own delicate, glasslike quality and says:

Has anyone ever told you that you were pretty? Well,
you are! In a very different way from anyone else. And
all the nicer because of the difference, too . . . I wish
that you were my sister. I'd teach you to have some confidence in yourself. The different people are not like
other people, but being different is nothing to be
ashamed of. Because other people are not such wonderful people. They're one hundred times one thousand.
You're one times one!

Laura had known Jim from a far and admiring distance
six years before when he was the high school hero, the
star in basketball, captain of the debating club, presi-
dent of the senior class and the glee club, and the male
singing lead in the annual light operas. She had sat
across from him in the auditorium on Mondays, Wednes-
days, and Fridays and once, when she had been absent,
he had asked her what was the matter; and when she
answered that she had been sick with pleurosis, Jim had
thought she said *blue roses* and that became the name he
called her through high school, his special name for her
shy, unobtrusive self—Blue Roses.

God, ever the Gentleman Caller, speaks our name; he
too personalizes his attentions. He whispers *beloved*,
and we know in one sense that this is a corporate endear-
ment, but we hear the words spoken singularly.

At a conference on spiritual growth, I led the group
into the prayer of listening, a practical training session in
how to be still, how to become silent in order to hear
God. One woman waited for me after the meeting ad-
journed. "I wanted to share with you," she said. "I was
sexually abused as a child, and it has been hard for me to
experience God's love. But while I was practicing the
prayer of listening just now, I heard him speak to my
heart, *You are my beloved.* I have never heard that before. I know that everyone is loved by him, but he spoke
those words as if I were his *only* beloved."

Like handsome Jim, gallant and light-hearted, who leaned in concern across the auditorium aisle, God leans close and calls us by our special name. He calls us when, crippled and disfigured, we clump awkwardly up the stairs, the noise embarrassing, sounding like thunder to. our own ears; and he calls that endearing name as we hide among the frail toys we allow to occupy us because we are too timid to face the realities and competitions of a harsh world. He showers us with flattering attentions. We blush, amazed to be suddenly the focus of his gaze. He watches us—jealously even—and moves perceptibly closer when others are near.

I believe that each boyfriend, each attentive male, each man who comes with love in his eyes, each gentleman caller is a type, a human picture of another gentlemanly beau, God. God is the ultimate Gentleman Caller, "the long delayed, but always expected something that we live for."

F. Scott Peck, the author of the best-selling *The Road Less Traveled*, said in a lecture that spirituality and sexuality arc so close it is impossible to speak of one without the other. My notes on that session read: God is the Divine Courter who is continually wooing us to his bed. And in its spiritual sense this is true; Christian divines invariably draw parallels between human and heavenly love; they know, by experience, God to be the lover of their souls.

In addition to all his other attributes, God is Love. He is a lover of the soul who woos each of us as though we were the only one.

It is in this context of God's attribute as Divine Lover that a great romance is dramatized. The script begins early in the Scriptures: "I am the Lord, . . . and I will take you for my people, and I will be your God . . ." (Exodus 6:6, 7). These words are spoken to Israel, a slave girl of Egypt, under hard bondage, misused, abused—but suddenly favored, because the eye of a powerful lord has

noticed her, sees her potential beauty and is determined
to loose her bonds. It is as though he has said, "I will be
your man, and you will be my woman."

In the book *The Divine Romance,* author Gene Edwards writes of Israel, "In the eyes of earthen man she
was a nation, but through the eyes of God a woman. A
nation, yes; but in His sight a composite woman . . . he
loved this one, visited, counseled her."

What a daring rescue he arranges for this slave maiden!
What a heroic master plan he executes—escape, chase,
deliverance. Moses wrote a song about it: "I will sing to
the Lord, for he has triumphed gloriously; the horse and
rider he has thrown into the sea. . . . Thou hast led in
thy steadfast love the people whom thou hast redeemed . . ." (Exodus 15:1, 13).

Sir Walter Scott captured the essence of breathless
last-minute deliverance in his romantic novel *Ivanhoe.*
The beautiful Jewess Rebecca, who has nursed the
wounded and disinherited Lord Wilfred of Ivanhoe
(falling in love with him, but hopelessly because of her
race) finds herself abducted by the Templar Knight,
Brian de Bois-Guilbert, whose seductive attentions she
has resolutely refused. Twisted circumstances, however,
inveigh against her. Due to the machinations of the
Grand Master of the Templar Knights, a malevolent fig-
ure, she is tried and condemned as a sorceress and sen-
tenced to die, to burn at the stake. Fate twists: Rebecca's
captor, now under orders from the evil Grand Master,
has become, despite his own wishes, her accuser.

Scott captures the pageantry and language of these
heraldic times. The trumpets flourish. The herald cries.

But no champion appears for the beautiful Rebecca
who is offered a last chance to admit her guilt and obtain
pardon. She refuses. (A delay is granted for one hour,
and all await the young woman's fate.) Finally, at the last
moment, his horse fatigued from hard riding, a champion appears, but either from weariness or weakness, he

can scarcely support himself in the saddle. It is Ivanhoe, barely healed, who proclaims, "I am a good knight and noble, come hither to sustain with lance and sword the just and lawful quarrel of this damsel, Rebecca . . . and to defy Sir Brian de Bois-Guilbert, as a traitor, murderer, and liar; as I will prove in this field with my body against his. . . ."

The Grand Master holds in his hand the gage of battle, the doomed maiden's glove; he throws it down to the fatal signal words, *Laissez aller.* The knights charge. The wearied horse and rider go down before the well-aimed lance of the Templar Knight, but to the astonishment of all, Bois-Guilbert also reels in his saddle, looses his stirrups and falls in the lists. Untouched, he dies; a judgment of God. The maiden is pronounced free and guiltless.

Ivanhoe is a classic sample of the romantic form of literature, often overblown with sentimentalism and awash with idealism, but it lends a parallel portrayal of the drama of the love story of a God and a people, a Divine Deliverer who rescues his loved one from the clutches of another evil Grand Master, the Pharaoh. He frees her, this one called Israel, bruised, chaffed, frightened, brutalized from bondage; and then this great lord most tenderly declares again, "And I will make my abode among you, and my soul shall not abhor you. And I will walk among you, and will be your God, and you shall be my people. I am the Lord your God, who brought you forth out of the land of Egypt, that you should not be their slaves; and I have broken the bars of your yoke and made you walk erect" (Leviticus 26:11–13).

The deliverance turns into a holy courtship, and the Divine Deliverer begins to define a betrothal agreement. He, the great lord, a most commanding potentate, is proposing marriage to the former slave girl of lowly nomadic origin. If she will set herself aside for him; if she will refuse to keep company with other men, and seek no other lovers; if she will learn to love him with her whole heart, soul, and strength; if she will pledge herself to live a life different from all the other slave girls of common derivation, then he will covenant to be her husband, to betroth her to himself, to bless her with his riches, to endow her with his royal inheritance, to marry her at a future date, to celebrate the wedding feast at a gathering of the nations of the world, and to keep the marital love warm, living, eternally lasting.

In this sense, the Old Testament records a romance: The One Great Lord chooses a pitiful young woman because he sees her potential beauty; he falls in love with her, draws her in merciful compassion into his arms, wipes the tears from her cheeks, and speaks her special name, whispering that he has chosen her for his bride. And she is to follow him the rest of her days.

He gives her a ring to wear, the gold band of Sabbath that will remind her of this betrothal covenant, a sign to all the other lords that she is engaged to the One Great Lord.

All love stories, whether ancient or modern, whether fiction or true, are but pale imitations, impoverished comparisons to this cosmic drama which begins on the stage of the Old Testament and continues with a "second act" performed on the platform of the New. Here a worthy human woman bears God's Son, a manchild who takes on flesh to continue the wooing in a way that can be seen. He, too, is "the long delayed but always expected something that we wait for," the Gentleman Caller, now in human form.

Ironically, when grown, he performs his first rites of divinity at a marriage feast, turning the water to wine for the wedding celebrants. He, too, finally becomes a deliverer, a champion, and proves a rightful challenger in the field Calvary against the tempter, the traitorous seducer, the Grand Master of evil. He redeems his beloved, the world, at all cost, with his own body as forfeit.

To miss this motif of the Divine Romance embossed upon the Old and New Testament is to miss God's love scheme and to be unprepared for the last and final act— the marriage celebration of the wedding of the bride and the Bridegroom. It is to be an unready virgin, without enough oil to keep her lamp burning until the Lord finally comes.

And to misunderstand this love scheme is also to misunderstand the role of Sabbath. For Sabbath is the ring a loving God, the Divine Wooer, gives his chosen one to wear; it is a gold band to remind her, through the long days of waiting, of his betrothal covenant—a sign to her and to all the other eager young lords, the overly attentive suitors, that she is engaged to, set apart for, this One Great Lord. She belongs to Him.

13

The Ring

I HAVE CHANGED MY MIND about engagement rings. When I was a freshman in college (seventeen years of age) being swept off my feet by an older man (seven years my senior), I thought it was crass to measure one's love by a thing so material as the size of a diamond. Many of the girls on Wheaton College campus were receiving diamonds, but a simple gold wedding band exchanged in the marriage ceremony would suffice for me.

At least that's what I thought at the time, and I couldn't understand why David insisted on getting me an engagement ring. And yet I had understood perfectly his nonverbal message as he ushered me out of my parents' home one spring evening while a group of young men from the freshmen dormitory gathered on the lawn to serenade. Handsome in a white dinner jacket, David had parked his car at the curb, called for me at the door, then marched me through the crew of younger men, several of whom I had been dating. His decisiveness proclaimed territorial rights—I got that much, and so did the serenaders—they never sang beneath my window again.

So despite my youthful idealism, I acquiesced to David's wishes, and we went shopping for a diamond.

Because I was so young, we headed into Chicago. David was my Youth for Christ director, a college graduate with seminary training; I was scarcely out of high school. The city provided an anonymity lacking in our small town with many familiar eyes. The jewelry store we chose was situated smack-dab on a bustling corner of State Street right in the heart of the Loop. Please notice the past tense; it shortly went out of business for reasons which will soon become obvious.

Proudly, David escorted me into the gaudy showroom where an eager-beaver salesman soon had us signing a contract on the dotted line. We chose a modest-sized ring which suited our limited financial circumstances, put down a deposit and ransomed a good share of our future weekly budget to this fast-talking diamond dealer.

Upon returning home, however, David thought twice about his purchase and marched me (again) into the local and very trustworthy jewelry store on Front Street in downtown Wheaton for an outside appraisal. Mr. Stone, the owner of the store, peered through his eyeglass at the pledge of my one true love and pronounced the stone flawed and quite a few points smaller than what the downtown city-slicker salesman had guaranteed.

Now what were we to do? We had signed on the dotted line. Our love would be forever measured by this inadequate token; an omen, perhaps, of future disappointment.

At this point, my mother-in-law-to-be came to the rescue. Unaware of our woebegone straits, she took one look at the ring and said to David, "I'd be ashamed to give a diamond that small to the girl I loved. You take it back and exchange it for a bigger stone."

That's exactly what David did.

Emboldened by the effect of maternal disapproval, he walked into that slick downtown diamond merchandiser in Chicago and announced to the shyster salesman, "My mother thinks this stone is too small. We'd like to return this ring and buy something larger." Eagerly, the salesman cancelled the contract, returned the deposit, and we did buy a larger ring—from Mr. Stone (such an appropriate name!), the friendly neighborhood jeweler on Front Street in Wheaton, Illinois.

Was an engagement ring worth all this trouble?

It seems to have been worth all the trouble to David. For despite the mutuality of modern marriages, despite the team ministry we have since carefully forged, courtship and engagement is a period in which territorial prerogatives are clearly established. An engagement ring firmly declares: This woman is taken. These two have pledged to each other loving fidelity.

God is a Divine Lover wooing a people. The prophet Hosea makes the Lord's intent implicitly clear, "And in that day . . . you will call me, 'My husband,' and no longer will you call me, 'My Baal.' . . . And I will betroth you to me for ever; I will betroth you to me in righteousness and in justice, in steadfast love, and in mercy. I will betroth you to me in faithfulness; and you shall know the Lord" (Hosea 2:16, 19). Isaiah also tells Israel, "For your Maker is your husband, the Lord of hosts is his name . . ." (Isaiah 54:5).

During the Old Testament betrothal period, God gives a ring to his beloved, an engagement ring, if you please, so that she will have a pledge of his enduring love and a reminder that she belongs to him. That ring is the Sabbath.

Exodus 3:13 says, "You shall keep my sabbaths, for this is a sign between me and you throughout your generations, that you may know that I, the Lord, sanctify you."

In my reading on the Jewish Sabbath I discovered writings by Rabbi Abraham Heschel that said, "In the Friday evening service we say, 'Thou has sanctified the seventh day,' referring to the marriage of the bride to the groom. In Hebrew, *sanctification* is the word for marriage."

The Hebrew word for sanctification *(le-kadesh)* is the same as the word for marriage.

I'm no Hebrew scholar; nevertheless, I went back and looked at all the scriptures regarding the Sabbath that used the word *sanctify,* and in these passages, I substituted the word *marriage.* Now the Exodus passage becomes meaningful in relationship to the love motif, "You shall keep my sabbaths, for this is a sign between me and you, throughout your generations, that you may know that I, the Lord, sanctify you [am married unto you]."

The giving of the ring is the most important act of the entire Jewish wedding ceremony. The groom puts the ring on the index finger of the bride's right hand and recites: "Behold you are consecrated to me with this ring according to the Law of Moses and Israel."

The Jewish Catalog digresses at this point in its explanation of marriage customs (and throws some light onto the declaration of the prophet Ezekiel) by emphasizing: "This statement is the essence of the ceremony and legalizes the marriage. All the rest is deeply rooted in tradition and plays a significant role in the overall ritual of ceremony but possesses no legal status. It is *crucial* to understand the seriousness of this act. A marriage has taken place *halakhically* anytime:

(a) a man hands a woman an object worth more than one penny; and (b) she accepts it knowingly; and (c) he recites 'Behold you are consecrated to me with this ring according to the Law of Moses and Israel.'; and (d) there are at least two acceptable witnesses.

"And this means anywhere, anytime, with or without a rabbi, license, huppah, etc. No one should joke around with this ritual."

Being sanctified before the Lord, or being holy as unto him, or being set apart for him is hard for me to understand; but if I say, my relationship to him is as though I'm married to him, and keeping the Sabbath is a sign of this, a celebration that I enact so I will not forget, so I will be reminded of this holy union—then suddenly, being sanctified takes on a mental image I can better comprehend. I know what it means to be married. As a wife of twenty-five years, I know what it means to give myself to another, to not desire any other, to live my life around another, to put the good of that person before my own good.

Observing Sabbath is like wearing an engagement ring. This ring we wear in weekly celebration not only reminds us that we're married to another (or betrothed with the same seriousness as in a marital covenant); it's not only a symbolic seal that binds us to our vows of spiritual fidelity, but Sabbath-keeping is the ring we put on that protects us from the seducing attentions of this evil world.

This was illustrated for me one summer day when my daughter and I drove into Chicago to attend the Tiffany Glass Exhibit which had been mounted at the Museum of Natural History. Melissa invited a close friend and her mother to go with us, and we stopped to have breakfast at a favorite eating place in the city.

This particular restaurant is not much on decor, it's definitely the chrome-and-plastic-upholstery variety, but it's always filled with patrons of local Chicago color. The aged owner meets you at the door and gives kisses (and boxes of Milk Duds) to the female clientele.

The whole establishment is filled with wonderful incongruities, reason enough for me to patronize the place; but in addition, the food is fabulous and reasonable.

Located close to the train stations, a line often stretches down the block from the restaurant while commuters make a breakfast stop on their way to work.

Fortunately for us, on the morning of our Tiffany-outing we had only a short wait; but in that time, the maitre d' became surprisingly flirty and attempted to match us up with the single men in the line ahead of us.

How does one fend off unwelcome over-attentive males?

Actually, we didn't have to. The nice looking young man in the line ahead of us took a quick glance at our ring fingers and said to the maitre d', "Oh, I think I'll pass. They're wearing wedding rings. I stay away from married women."

Looking back, I can see that the young man was glad of a way out of an awkward predicament. I know I certainly was relieved to have been spared potential embarrassment; but because of this incident, I've considered the thousands of miles I've traveled by myself across this country and internationally, into airports and out of airports, hailing taxis in unfamiliar cities, finding the right courtesy limousines to take me to convention hotels, walking in unlikely neighborhoods in strange cities, and it is wonderful to me that I have never been accosted by a too-interested male stranger.

I wonder how many unknown glances there have been through the years at my ring finger adorned with its simple gold band and the engagement diamond my husband insisted on giving me when I was a freshman in college? How efficiently they have silently signaled, *this woman is taken*.

When discussing the idea of sanctification as holy betrothal, of God to a people or to us as individuals, it is important to understand ancient Jewish marriage customs as contrasted to our culture in which a young woman is engaged on an average as often as three times. According to what Alfred Edersheim writes in *Sketches of Jewish Social Life in the Days of Christ,* "From the moment of her betrothal, a woman was treated as if she were actually married. The union could not be dissolved, except by regular divorce; a breach of faithfulness was regarded as adultery; and the property of the woman became virtually that of her betrothed, unless he had expressly renounced it. . . ." He points out that the Mishnah (early written Jewish authority) describes regular writings of betrothal which stipulated the mutual obligations, the dowry, and all other points on which the parties had agreed. The author feels that it is safe to conclude that these New Testament betrothal customs were derivative from Old Testament customs and similar in their formality.

The betrothal, in ancient Jewish culture, therefore, was a legally formalized, seriously bonding premarital pact. Even today, betrothal is considered a serious undertaking among observant Jewry. The agreement of *tenaim,* a written legal betrothal contract, is still considered binding on both parties, as binding in the Jewish mind as a marriage contract—only dissoluble through divorce or death. The old tradition, however, has been circumscribed by modern pragmatism with the traditional custom of signing it a year before the wedding giving way, in general, to signing it immediately before the ceremony.

So God calls a people (Israel) to be his corporate bride, he makes a solemn love covenant with them and gives them a betrothal ring which they are to wear, the Sabbath; and this is a binding agreement which does not have the casual implications of engagements in modern Western culture, but one in which the woman is considered already married.

God is an artist who paints pictures of himself in the world. And one of the pictures he has painted shows physical married love as a symbol of his own love for humankind. The Song of Solomon, if anything, is a celebration of sexuality, again playing on the themes of romance, betrothal, physicality, and marriage, "While the king was on his couch, my nard gave forth its fragrance. My beloved is to me a bag of myrrh, that lies between my breasts" (Song of Solomon 1:12, 13). In a sense, this book of Scripture is a collection of erotic poetry made holy by the marriage bed and its allegorical relationship to God and his covenanted people.

This analogy is also strongly underlined in Jewish Sabbath traditions.

As mentioned in earlier chapters, by orthodox Jewish understanding, Sabbath is observed from sundown Friday evening to sundown Saturday evening. The Friday evening meal is a celebration of creation and of the Creator, and it is strongly rooted in the sensual, in the beauty of linen cloths, and matched china, of silver settings and flowers, of specially prepared food and waxy candlelight, of the tantalizing smell of wine and the *challot*, yeasty braided bread, of clean rooms and fresh clothes, of shining hair and bathed bodies.

The Jewish Catalog states: "The basic theme of Friday night is creation. . . . In our observance of the Shabbat, we bear witness to and affirm the creation. Specifically, on Friday the creation motif appears in the Kiddush, in certain references in the Evening Service, in songs, and also in the propitiousness of intercourse with one's spouse."

In the Barbra Streisand–produced film *Yentl*, based on an Isaac Bashevis Singer story with an implausible plot, a young Jewish girl (Yentl) disguises herself as a boy student (Anschul) and through improbable machinations marries her/his best friend's (Avigdor's) sweetheart (Haddas)! After circuitous subterfuges, Haddas implores Anschul to the bed late one afternoon by saying, "It's almost sundown—Sabbath. Mother says it's a special blessing to make love on the Sabbath."

This poignant and lovely phrase has stayed in my mind, "It's a special blessing to make love on the Sabbath." Human love is a symbol of the Creator's love.

In *The Sabbath* (Burning Bush Press, 1970, p. 26), Rabbi Samuel Dresner states, "It is possible for the Jew to fall in love with the Sabbath itself. . . . It is the peculiar inward feeling of the Jew which characterizes the Sabbath day, a feeling of love, devotion, and joy."

The Decalogue declares, "Remember the sabbath day, to keep it holy" (Exodus 20:8).

There are many theological explanations for Sabbath-keeping. In fact, the more I study and the more I learn and the more I practice, the more I agree with Karl Barth's exclamation of "a certain awe, the radical importance, the almost monstrous range of the Sabbath commandment. . . . This commandment is total. It discovers and claims man in his depths and from his utmost bounds." Yet no theology stimulates me motivationally more than the love analogy. Once, the day set aside for the Lord used to be the worst day of days for me, but this particular understanding is helping Sunday to become a wonderful day, in fact the best day of the week.

For I am learning to observe Sunday with a Sabbath heart, with the heart of a young woman who polishes her engagement ring, who holds it to the light so the diamond can catch the shining, who remembers that the keeping of this day is meaningful to the One she loves, whose heart floods with joy at the thought that *he* is coming in a special way, that the day will be spent in his company without the distractions of the workweek.

I look inward and make sure there are no idol suitors vying for my attention. Is my heart chaste? Have my thoughts been for my Loved One and for him alone? Is there anything in my life that will cause him grief when we come together?

And I am learning that Sabbath is a love day, a day to adore. As I strive to celebrate Sunday with a Sabbath heart, I have learned that when the Loved One is near, I don't work. This is a day set apart for loving.

And each Sabbath/Sunday (Saturday evening to Sunday evening) I touch these real rings upon my finger, the gold engagement ring with its diamond which David gave me to establish his love proprietorship and the wedding band. I turn them and think of the symbolic ring (Sabbath/Sunday) and how it says to a seducing world, "This woman (this man) is betrothed to, married to, set apart for, saved for, sanctified unto Another." The wearing of this ring, like the ones David gave me, reminds me that I am not my own. The wearing of it says to all those others attempting to capture my attentions, "She is keeping her oath of betrothal; she is learning to live out a sacred vow to God . . . *to thee only will I cling.*"

14

Mental Fidelity

ORTHODOX JEWS WRAP themselves in a prayer shawl, the *tallit*, where even the fringe (the *tzitzit*) is knotted ritualistically to represent letters in the Hebrew alphabet which stand for the name of God. An old meditation reminds the Jew of the symbolic meaning of being wrapped in this cloth during prayer—*For the purpose of unifying the Holy One . . . for the purpose of unifying the YH of God's Name* [masculine] *with the VH of God's Name* [feminine] *in one complete Unity, in the name of all Israel, I wrap myself in this tallit with tzitzit.*

Even in the custom of the prayer shawl, we see that God is involved in the sexuality of his people.

"So God created man in his own image, in the image of God he created him; male and female he created them" (Genesis 1:27). Man and woman together, complementary and compatible, are a fleshly investiture of God's nature.

"It is good!" God shouts like all pleased creators standing aside to examine the finished product. "It is good!" Here was the original utopia of order and harmony where the culmination of his creative powers, man and woman, could live. In this most exquisite garden God would be their friend and walk beside them and they would love him and love each other.

It is during this idyllic genesis epoch that we are told God rested on the seventh day—"And on the seventh day God finished his work which he had done, and he rested on the seventh day . . . So God blessed the seventh day and hallowed it . . ." (Genesis 2:2, 3). God rested but not from weariness. He neither needs slumber nor sleep. He rested because he was satisfied with his creative work. The perfect world had been created. It was good. So he established a memorial to this perfect work, not an engraved plaque hammered to Eden's gates—*here lies the perfect place*—but a weekly reminder to rest; and he invites his creation, man and woman, to observe this perpetual time marker.

"Remember the sabbath day, to keep it holy." The commandment is birthed in the wonder of God's love, not as a legalistic obligation, and it is important to interpret this injunction in terms of that love, and not of legality if we are not to lose its essential meaning.

But God's grand design is spoiled. Temptation rolls its eyes and rubs its hands. Innocence is betrayed; the serpent slithers away only to come another day. The loved ones are expelled from Paradise; angels guard the entrance with flaming swords to prevent rehabitation. The Man and Woman's garden walks with God are over. He can no longer look on his created things and call them good.

Infidelity, unfaithfulness of one kind or another, always destroys the utopias, the better worlds we long for.

This is poignantly illustrated by the modern rendition of the Camelot legend, *The Once and Future King,* by

T. H. White. Arthur, tutored by the magician Merlyn, has a better idea for English history. He explains it to a young French lad, Lancelot, who seems to be winning most of the games. "I want to get hold of a lot of people who are good at games, to help with an idea I have. It is for the time when I am a real King, and have got this kingdom settled. . . . It is about knights. I want to have an order of Chivalry . . . which goes about fighting against Might. . . . Do you understand what I am talking about?"

The lad understands, "We call it Fort Mayne in France. The man with the strongest arm in a clan gets made the head of it, and does what he pleases. . . . You want to put an end to the Strong Arm, by having a band of knights who believe in justice rather than strength. Yes, I would like to be one of those very much. I must grow up first. Thank you. Now I must say goodby."

The encounter with Arthur is short, but life-changing. A dream begins growing in the young lad's heart. "He wanted to be the best knight in the world, so that Arthur would love him in return, and he wanted one other thing which was still possible in those days. He wanted, through his purity and excellence, to be able to perform some ordinary miracle—to heal a blind man or something like that, for instance."

Arthur is a king who enters English history at a time when Might rules with an unjust and rapacious iron hand. A visionary, he dreams of a better world to be governed by the Knights of the Round Table. But all utopias are ruined by the seeds of destruction which lie dormant and brooding in the very people who dare to dream of better ways.

Man can conceive of better worlds; he just cannot sustain them. Infidelity always enters—unfaithfulness to the original intent, abandonment of the corporate ideal for the sake of personal gain, coveting another's love for one's own. All grand designs—whether governments,

new societies, communal experiments, perfect unions—
are spoiled. Chaos clamors. War and malignancy stalk.
The brief shining moments of all the Camelots of all
times are extinguished to become legends, stories, history, memories.

Lancelot, now a man, the best knight in the world,
beloved by the king, despite mighty inward strivings,
begins an affair with Queen Guenever, Arthur's cherished wife. Their unfaithfulness blossoms with forbidden fruit the plucking of which threatens to dismember
Camelot. Mordred, the king's illegitimate son, moth-
ered by Arthur's own half-sister, the beautiful witch
Morgeuse, grasps ill-fated opportunity; he accuses the
two lovers of treason, and appeals beyond the rule of
just might to Arthur's laboriously constructed new idea,
the rule of law.

The infidelity is proven, the kingdom is dismembered,
the opposing parties are plunged into war, Mordred
grabs the power to rule and proposes himself as king and
husband to Guenever. Arthur dies on a field in England,
having returned from France, before he can rescue his
guilty queen. A spoiler has been loosed upon Camelot;
and Camelot itself is spoiled.

Like all the Arthurs of one kind or another to come,
like all the visionary utopians ever after, God had a
grand design for the world. It was transgressed by infidelity; the garden consequently barred. But God is ever
the originator, the tenacious conceptualizer, the creator
of eternal regenesis; he begins again. He chooses another to cherish.

God takes pains to make his love relationship known.
"And you shall be my people, and I will be your God," is
a statement which occurs at least twenty-eight times
in the Old and New Testament and is often followed by
covenant agreements, promises which are similar to
those vows we offer at wedding ceremonies.

Most wedding vows include a phrase of promised

fidelity. *The Minister's Service Book,* which I borrowed from my husband's library shelves, includes several ceremonies, all of which include some form of the promise to love, comfort, honor, and keep in sickness and in health; and, forsaking all others, keep thee only unto you, so long as we both shall live.

Of course, both the bride and the bridegroom always respond affirmatively. I can't imagine a wedding ceremony where one or the other would equivocate, "Well, comfort, honor, and keep in sickness and in health— that's OK; but forsaking all others?—I think I'll hedge my bets a bit on that one."

All promise. Yet fidelity seems to be one of the hardest of vows to keep. Witness the literature of the world, witness the television media; researchers tell us that 80 percent of all sexual acts inferred or portrayed on television are outside the context of marriage. An hour or two of listening to country/western music's moanful wailing over broken vows, philandering women, and womanizing gents summarizes in down-to-earth terms the mourner's dirge over the gravesite of a once-promised faithful love.

Orthodox Jews, almost obsessively, remind themselves of God's fidelity agreement with man. Phylacteries are boxes tied on the head and arm every weekday morning, during Shaharit—morning prayers. This activity is seen as a response to various commands from the Pentateuch such as "bind them as a sign upon your hand, and they shall be as frontlets between your eyes" (Deuteronomy 6:8). Leather cords attach to these tefillin (phylacteries) and wrap around the head and around the forearm and hand. The Jew repeats the *Shema* as he binds these prayer reminders to himself, "Hear O Israel, the Lord your God, the Lord is One. And you shall love the Lord your God with all your heart, and with all your soul, and with all your might. . . ." The binding continues as the strap is wound and these verses are repeated from Hosea, "And I will betroth you to me for ever . . . and you shall know the Lord . . ." (2:19, 20).

The verb translated "know" in this verse refers to an experiential rather than an academic understanding. For example, this word is also used to mean sexual intercourse, the most intimate kind of human knowing. It is this kind of profound experiential knowing that Hosea meant and of which the practicing Jew seeks to remind himself through ritual enactment.

God intended himself to be known by his people intimately. After the first ancient disaster, he would come again and dwell among them, they would begin to create another nearly perfect world, ". . . he will love you, bless you, and multiply you; he will also bless the fruit of your body and the fruit of your ground, your grain and your wine and your oil, the increase of your cattle and the young of your flock, in the land which he swore to your fathers to give you. You shall be blessed above all peoples; there shall not be male or female barren among you, or among your cattle. And the Lord will take away from you all sickness and none of the evil diseases of Egypt, which you knew, will he inflict upon you . . ." (Deuteronomy 7:13–15). All these rich promises are contingent upon the Israelites keeping their covenant vows of fidelity.

David and I have interpreted our wedding vows of fidelity to include meanings even more profound than just physical fidelity, a faithfulness of the body; we interpret them to mean that in our marriage we will also practice mental fidelity, a faithfulness of the mind. We will not think romantically of someone else; we will not mull over the attractions of the opposite sex in a way that takes precedence over the favors of our own spouse; we will not allow our minds to focus in sexual attraction on any other human other than our mate.

"That's even harder yet," people reply when we teach about mental fidelity.

Obviously, like any other discipline, establishing the discipline of fidelity is work; but once established, a good habit is as hard to break as a bad one. "It is not your love that sustains the marriage; but from now on, the marriage that sustains your love," writes Dietrich Bonhoeffer, and David quotes him with each wedding ceremony he performs. Commitment as expressed in not only physical, but also mental faithfulness, binds the marriage. Trust grows, confidence in the long-lasting love of one's husband or wife; never needing to worry in the presence of members of the opposite sex, security, safety, contentment flourish.

What's "truly harder yet" is trying to make a marriage work when the vows of faithfulness do not include an understanding of mental fidelity. That's rough work.

It is not until I begin to practice mental fidelity that I can truly understand the spiritual fidelity that God requires of a people who desire to serve and follow him. I firmly believe that the quality of my mental and physical fidelity toward my husband and his toward me is a sign of the quality of my spiritual fidelity for God. This is the prayer shawl I pull tightly about me—if I am unfaithful to my husband in any way, the spiritual bonds of promise begin to loosen; if I am unfaithful to God in any way, the earthly bonds of promise begin to loosen. This symbol of my love for God, my human marriage, is intrinsically interwoven with the spiritual marriage of my soul— God's unity, the YH combined with the VH is interlinked with the anima and the animus (the feminine and masculine) of my own self and of that of my mate.

Strangely, Lancelot strives mightily with this understanding as portrayed in *The Once and Future King*. He fails, but the concept is succinctly expressed. "The Ill-Made Knight was not involved in an Eternal Triangle. It was an Eternal Quadrangle." Whether we know it or not, our fidelities and our infidelities always involve that unseen Presence, a holy God.

So Israel was betrothed to her Husband, promising to live out holy lives before him, and a weekly sign of this intense betrothal relationship would be Sabbath observance—not just a formulated ritual, but a day of adoration and expressed, spoken love where time was set aside, different from all the other days of the week, to enjoy the company of the Beloved in a special way. God would not stand far off, but would come close to them in their very acts of love, in their worship of him. And they would give unto him a spiritual fidelity of heart, soul, and might.

The concept of sanctification as 'being married unto' helps me understand why the prophets regularly spoke of Israel's idolatry in terms of sexual infidelity. Listen to Jeremiah whose descriptions of spiritual adultery are almost embarrassingly graphic, "I remember the devotion of your youth, your love as a bride, how you followed me in the wilderness in a land not sown. Israel was holy to the Lord [or Israel was betrothed, was married to the Lord]. . . . long ago you broke your yoke and . . . said, 'I will not serve.' Yea, upon every high hill and under every green tree you bowed down as a harlot. . . . Look at your way in the valley; . . . a restive young camel interlacing her tracks, a wild ass used to the wilderness, in her heat sniffing the wind! Who can restrain her lust? None who seek her need weary themselves; in her month they will find her" (Jeremiah 2:2–3, 20–24).

Again, an expulsion, the loved one is cast out of a land flowing with milk and honey. She has defied her love covenant. She has worshiped other gods; she has defiled the new utopia with brutal injustice. Israel is dispersed. Exiled. The vow of love has been shattered; the blessing from the practice of fidelity withdrawn. She becomes captive to a cruel and terrorizing warlord, Babylon. The beauty loses her lustre, covered with sores, the once shining eyes are matted with crust, her hair falls out in patches. A dirge wails, a lamentation rises, "I have forsaken my house, I have abandoned my heritage; I have given the beloved of my soul into the hands of her enemies" (Jeremiah 12:7). The holy husband weeps again over the broken unity of his love relationship with his people.

But with incredible tenacity, God begins again. A manchild is born, a promised, long-expected one, the divine human. A new community is in the making, a kingdom like no other, one which will be ruled by a benevolent dictator, this King Jesus. And the church will be his people, the new bride he is forming for himself. This time, the Lover walks among them, in the flesh; he can be seen, touched, heard, observed; he calls them to the old, broken betrothal vows. They are to love God with their heart, mind, and strength; and their neighbor as themselves. He becomes the Champion for them against the old Spoiler; he gives them his own Holy Spirit to teach them how to love him and how to love each other. But the tendency to despoil, to be unfaithful lies lurking. The apostle Paul warns the New Testament church, "I feel a divine jealousy for you, for I betrothed you to Christ to present you as a pure bride to her one husband. But I am afraid that as the serpent deceived Eve by his cunning, your thoughts will be led astray from a sincere and pure devotion to Christ" (2 Corinthians 11:2–3).

So now the centuries have passed and we stand in the Christian era, and the majority of us observe a day set aside for expressing our love—Sunday, the Lord's Day we call it—but something is wrong. For many of us, this is the worst day of the week. It's fatiguing, filled with ennui as we sit in church pews and listen to sermons; and often it is characterized by an inner, unstated dread. Our thoughts are being led astray from a sincere and pure devotion to Christ. How often we would like just to stay home, and how often many of us do.

We have become like the dutiful wives described in *Revival Lectures* long ago by the preacher Charles G. Finney

> A backslider in heart finds his religious duties a burden to him. He has promised to serve the Lord. He dare not wholly break from the form of service, and he tries to be dutiful, while he has no heart in prayer, in praise, in worship, or in any of those exercises which are so spontaneous and delightful, where there is true love to God. The backslider in heart is often like a dutiful, and unloving wife. She tries to do her duty to her husband, but fails utterly because she does not love him. Her painstaking to please her husband is constrained, not the spontaneous outburst of a loving heart; and her relationship and her duties become the burden of her life. She goes about complaining of the weight of care that is upon her, and will not be likely to advise young ladies to marry. She is committed for life, and must therefore perform the duties of married life, but it is such a bondage!

And the church gathers to worship on Sunday—but can't wait until the service ends. And it sits by habit, sings hymns by rote, bows its head as customary but thinks of other things—houses to furnish and clothes to buy, and Sunday afternoon football, and how long before we get out of here, and Monday's responsibilities and the children. But we hardly think of *him*, this Divine Lover who waits for our ardent, joyous attention, who is constantly wooing us to his bed. How weary he must be of the infinite varieties of mankind's infidelities! What anguish he must experience as he watches us despoil his perfect plans! And God is in mourning again, watching the Spoiler as he pimps prostitution, as he seeks to divert the attention of the Lord's betrothed to other lovers.

What would Christ say if he were asked (if anyone

cared to ask him) about modern Christendom's Sunday worship?

I think he would say: *Though we have a relationship, the church is no longer good at making love and now even on Sunday, my love day, I know she's thinking about other suitors.*

We need to understand that when our attention is drawn constantly to something other than this Lord, when anything comes before our first, fresh love for God, we are in danger of idolatry. If we love anything more than we love him, our worship is fixed in another direction. What do we really think about on Sunday mornings? On what do our thoughts center? Physical infidelity always begins in the mind. Christ taught, "You have heard that it was said, 'You shall not commit adultery.' But I say to you that everyone who looks at a woman lustfully has already committed adultery with her in his heart." The same is true with spiritual adultery; it begins with mental wanderings, with hidden idolatry.

And when Sabbath ceases to be a sign, when we neglect bringing a Sabbath understanding to our Lord's Day observances, when the day is really like any other day, although like a dutiful wife, we go through the forms of love, it is as though we have taken off our wedding band and hidden it in a kitchen drawer. We are in danger of becoming the wife who is no longer even dutiful in her love-making, the woman who all the other women on the block know is carrying on an illicit affair, sneaking off to motels in the afternoon.

We are like this woman—another love has taken precedence in our lives.

15

The
Bridal
Procession

WEDDINGS CAN BE FUNNY AFFAIRS. When I recall
all the events that surrounded mine, it's amazing that the
wedding ties have lasted. Almost everything went wrong
that could go wrong, starting with the basic premise for
ceremonies. My mother wanted a big showy church wedding and I wanted a small, private celebration. So we
compromised—and had a big church wedding!

This is not so unusual in itself, many a young bride has
been wed in the same kind of traditional affair with
friends and family all in attendance; but what complicated these grand plans was that my parents never spent
money for anything they didn't have to. Thriftiness was a
point of pride, meaning that nothing was ever hired out;
all tasks from household repairs to weddings were homemade.

Take my wedding dress for instance. I had vowed that
my Gram, an accomplished seamstress, was not going to

wear herself out sewing. Fortunately, I was able to find a sample dress (which wedding shops have for prospective brides to try on in order to see which styles they prefer) made of beautiful lace and satin for only thirty dollars. Never mind that the bodice was two sizes too large and needed alteration. Never mind that the hem was several inches too long and there were some thirty yards of fabric in the three layers of the skirt and that my little Gram, on her hands and knees, hand-stitched every inch. I think I should have begun to suspect something was amiss in our approach when one day I heard her sigh, "Do you know, Karen Sue, I think it would have been easier to make you a dress from scratch."

And then there was the wedding cake which an acquaintance was contracted to bake and decorate for a most reasonable fee. The only problem was that she didn't provide delivery service and it poured rain the afternoon before our evening wedding when my future father-in-law and my husband-to-be struggled to move that gargantuan mountain of flour and sugar and frosting from her house into the back seat of their business station wagon. The cake slipped, and Dad hollered, "Catch the cake!" and although David prevented disaster, he discovered that there is no convenient means to steady a wobbling wedding cake.

I slept on the couch the night before my wedding day because we needed all our bedrooms for great-aunts and great-uncles. (My father would never have thought of housing kin in a motel.)

David was up until three in the morning the night before our wedding, finishing his work in order to take a three-day honeymoon, and he was so busy running errands for my mother and attending rehearsals and rehearsal dinners that he didn't have time for a fresh shave for his own wedding. I had to go out into the rainstormy afternoon to pick mock orange blossoms so my little cousins could scatter petals on the aisle during the wedding march, and humidity always encourages my hair to express its individuality. Daddy stepped on my wedding gown as we were rounding the back pews, and Mother wasn't sure when to sit down after the bride had been given away so the guests stood for quite a while. The photographer took so long after the ceremony that by the time he was finished, most of our friends (all five hundred of them) were gone.

Then some young men took all the tires off our car, which we thought we had successfully hidden, and while we were waiting for a good friend to put the tires back on our car, these same young men came cheekily into our living room with the intention of kidnapping me. But my wonderful new brother-in-law let the air out of their tires, so David and I made a successful getaway unmolested.

We spent the three days of our honeymoon in a far-from-luxurious cabin in the woods working our heads off getting ready for the next two weeks, which were spent in a Bible conference where we were in charge of the children's program. We had two hundred children from babes in arms to junior-highers for two hours a day for seven days, and David and I did such a good job that our superiors invited us to take the same responsibility the following year.

That whole scenario was strangely prophetic of the entire future of my life with David Mains. There has been much hard work. There has rarely been enough money. There has certainly been little luxury. We have had to fight and struggle and "do ourselves" all of the dreams which have burned in our hearts and our souls. We have always had hundreds of people around when we would have preferred it to be just the two of us. Children and deadlines and responsibilities have threatened to kidnap our attention from each other, and it has frequently rained on our celebrations. We have often had to make room for a houseful of extended family, and we have sometimes tripped over each other walking down the aisles of our days.

But truthfully, none of this matters because we have loved each other. David and I survived the wedding and our love has survived the marriage. This union has made all the complications of married life well worth it.

Now we are at the point in my daughter's life where bridal magazines appear in her college room at school, in the stack of reading material in the back of her car; and this despite the fact that I have frequently whispered in her ear (a joking reaction to the experience of my own past), "You don't want a big church wedding, do you? Something small and intimate. Or better yet, why not just elope?" This has been of no avail; something about weddings appeals to the heart of most young women.

In a sense, getting ready for Sunday, week after week, is a lifelong preparation for a wedding—preparation to meet the Lord as our Bridegroom.

The great romance begun at the dawning of time between a Creator and his creatures is played out upon the final stage of history. God has continually wooed his people, beginning with the betrothal covenant of the Old Testament, continuing through the New Testament where God's love finally takes on flesh, and culminating in the Revelation where the Scriptures proclaim the final consummation of this love affair between the human and the divine, "Hallelujah! For the Lord our God the Almighty reigns. Let us rejoice and exult and give him the glory, for the marriage of the Lamb has come, and his Bride has made herself ready; it was granted her to be clothed with fine linen, bright and pure" (Revelation 19:6–8).

The perfect Edenic beginning for God's creation is over, ruined by infidelity; and mankind now waits with yearning in the imperfect middle, looking again for the arrival of the "long delayed but always expected something that we live for"—Christ. How frequently our

Lord referred to himself as the Bridegroom in the hearing of the Jewish people who understood something of the Old Testament covenant in terms of the betrothal motif.

The passage in Matthew 9 is a clear allusion to himself; "Why do we and the Pharisees fast, but your disciples do not fast?" asked the disciples of John. And Jesus answered, "Can the wedding guests mourn as long as the bridegroom is with them? The days will come, when the bridegroom is taken away from them, and then they will fast."

The New Testament teaching is that Christ, the Lamb of God, the *Agnus Dei*, will marry his bride, the church, at his second coming. And our relationship to him now is again akin to that of betrothal. In the Middle East, a marriage began (sometimes years before the actual ceremony) with betrothal, in which a man in the eyes of the community was as good as married to his betrothed. This union (as I've already mentioned) could only be dissolved by divorce such as when Joseph realized that Mary was with child and "resolved to divorce her quietly." Betrothal was considered complete except for the privilege of sexual intimacy.

But when finally the time for betrothal was ended, and the wedding ceremony was near, the bridegroom would leave his house which was the center of the festivities, and with all his friends—musicians, and celebrants, and dancers—he would make his way to the bride's house where a simple marriage ritual took place. Then, taking her by the hand, he would bring her back to his house for the wedding feast which would sometimes last for days.

Christ's parable of the ten virgins tells about waiting for the bridegroom in this context of the groom coming to the bride's house and taking her back to his own abode, "As the bridegroom was delayed, they all slumbered and slept. But at midnight there was a cry, 'Behold, the bridegroom! Come out to meet him.' Then all those maidens rose and trimmed their lamps. And the foolish said to the wise, 'Give us some of your oil, for our lamps are going out . . .'" Christ ends this tale by saying, "Watch therefore, for you know neither the day nor the hour."

A picture of another wedding procession is beautifully captured in the Nobel Prize–winning trilogy *Kristen Lavransdatter* by Sigrid Undset:

> Then Lavrans took the bride's hand and led her down to Erlend. The bridegroom lifted her to the saddle, and himself mounted. They stayed their horses, side by side, these two, beneath the bridal balcony, while the train began to form and ride out through the courtyard gate. First the priests . . . then came the groomsmen and the bridesmaids, pair by pair. And now 'twas for Erlend and her to ride forth. After them came the bride's parents, the kinsmen, friends and guests, in a long line down betwixt the fences to the highway. Their road for a long way onward was strewn with clusters of rowan-berries, branchlets of pine, and the last white dog-fennel of autumn, and folk stood thick along the waysides where the train passed by, greeting them with a great shouting.
> . . . just after sunset, the bridal train rode back to Jorundgaard. Through the first falling folds of darkness the bonfires shone out red from the courtyard of the bridal house. Minstrels and fiddlers were singing and making drums and fiddles speak as the crowd of riders drew near to the warm red glare of fires.

We, the church, are Christ's betrothed. We are as married to him as married can be; he is our loving Bridegroom, faithful and true; but there is some dimension of intimacy yet to be consummated. He will leave his Father's house and come to our house and take for his bride the church. He will secure his beloved and take the bride back to himself. The relationship will be consummated; complete intimacy will be gained. There will be a wedding feast in his Father's house to which invitations will be extended: "Write this," reports the apostle John about the words of the angel. "Blessed are those who are invited to the marriage supper of the Lamb." (Paradoxically, we are both beloved bride and welcome guest.)

But it is our duty as his beloved, to be ready by developing the habit of waiting. We must not forget our intended is coming. We must not allow the memory of his features to blur. We must keep his name upon our lips. We must not allow our love to fade.

Keeping Sunday with a Sabbath heart helps us to develop this discipline. Each Sunday, week in and week out, is a time we set aside for looking at the picture of the One we love—for re-reading his letters and listening to the voice from our memory whispering love. And we do this so that we will be ready when the "long delayed but always expected someone that we wait for" stands outside our gates in the company of merry making friends. He knocks at the door, his robust voice exultant in jubilee, and he speaks our name as though it were the only one. "Behold! I stand at the door and knock. If anyone hears my voice and open the door, I will come into him and sup with him and he with me." In that day, he will take us, marry us and bring us, so to speak, into his bed.

Sunday is a holy festival that foreshadows that one great celebration supper of the wedding feast of the bride and the Lamb. This concept of the married relationship was inherent to Jewish understanding. An ancient Jewish allegory states: After the work of creation was completed, the Seventh Day pleaded: Master of the Universe, all that Thou hast created is in couples; to every day of the week Thou gavest a mate; only I was left alone. And God answered: The Community of Israel will be your mate.

There are many ways to look at Sunday. It can be viewed as the first day of the week which we offer up as a firstfruit in time to the Lord. It can be considered, as we have done, to be a synthesis of the old with the new. Many express their faith within the context of the Christian community by observing Sabbath in the Jewish context, from Friday at sundown to Saturday at sundown. One woman, a converted Jew, who called herself a "fulfilled Hebrew" told me that this was the way she deepened the understanding of her Jewishness which had almost been lost before she became a Christian. And as at every point of doctrine, discussions still rage concerning Sabbath/Sunday celebration.

At some place in history, however, the traditional church made the first day of the week the focus of its weekly worship observance. *The Westminster Confession*, chapter 21, article 7, reads: "As it is of the law of nature, that in general, a due proportion of time be set apart for the worship of God; so, in his Word, by a positive, moral and perpetual commandment, binding all men in all ages, he hath particularly appointed one day in seven for a Sabbath, to be kept holy unto him: which, from the beginning of the world to the resurrection of Christ, was the last day of the week; and, from the resurrection of Christ was changed into the first day of the week."

I am content to leave doctrinal disputes regarding the day of Sabbath observance to the theologians. The point about which I am concerned is made in Nicholas Bownde's book *The Doctrine of the Sabbath* (enlarged and revised in 1606) which insists that the Sabbath originated in Eden and that the fourth commandment is a moral concept binding on both Jew and Christian. He urges Christians to observe Sunday as carefully as the Jews did their Sabbath.

I prefer to worship the Lord in this special way on Sunday because the symbolism of Christ with us through the power of the resurrection helps me hold to the reality of his coming again. The words of the liturgy from

The Book of Common Prayer during the weekly celebration of the Eucharist move me emotionally with layers of impact. The bread is broken, the celebrant proclaims: "Christ our Passover is sacrificed for us." And the people respond: "Therefore let us keep the feast."

There is no feast without the presence of the Lord. He, lithe and laughing, will ride into our lives, one wedding day; and we will look into the eyes of this One who has challenged the evil lover who wrongfully claimed us, and he will demand the tribute, ourselves, for which he once gave his own body as forfeit. He will hold out his hand and call us to his side, to the marriage ceremony which has been foretold throughout the centuries and of which every human wedding is a type. And we will take his hand in response and blush at his love and smile and he will make us utterly one with him.

Sunday, celebrated with delight, captures a taste of the distant future; it is a prophetic vision of what eternity spent in Christ's presence will be like. How dare we pull dour faces and downcast eyes. According to Levitical law, no fasting was allowed on Sabbath and even the seven-day period of mourning was interrupted for Sabbath observance. The one psalm specifically assigned in intertestament times to Sabbath worship, Psalm 92, is a song of thanksgiving, sung in festive mood with musical instruments, ". . . to the music of the lute and the harp, to the melody of the lyre."

In this same vein, Rabbi Abraham Heschel states, "unless one learns how to relish the taste of the Sabbath while still in this world, unless one is initiated in the appreciation of eternal life, one will be unable to enjoy the taste of eternity in the world to come." And John Calvin taught that "the Lord through the seventh day has sketched for his people the coming perfection of His Sabbath in the Last Day." In eighteenth-century America, Jonathan Edwards preached that the Sabbath, "a pleasurable and joyful day," was "an image of the future heavenly rest of the church."

We will rest in the embrace of the Beloved. Hebrews 4:9 promises, "So then, there remains a sabbath rest for the people of God." Christ himself began to prepare his people for this eternal embrace of love. "Come to me, all who labor and are heavy laden, and I will give you rest. Take my yoke upon you and learn from me; for I am gentle and lowly in heart, and you will find rest for your souls. For my yoke is easy, and my burden is light." This invitation from Matthew 11:28–30 was apparently delivered on a Sabbath. Christ seemed to be drawing a parallel to Sabbath rest and to the rest he offers mankind, a rest that will extend into eternity in the divine embrace, the intimate union of a holy love.

In truth, when the bride finally is brought into the household of the Bridegroom, every day will be Sabbath. Eternity will be a Sabbath without end. As we place this wedding ring of Sabbath upon our finger as a sign that we are betrothed to him, waiting the consummation of a final marriage act, we are remembering God's act of creation, his bold impregnation of a world with burgeoning life; we are remembering the redemptive creative work of Christ, his impregnation of souls with spiritual nativity; we are looking forward to a final re-creation, a perfect world in a perfect time, a utopia that can no longer be spoiled by infidelity.

I am a middle-aged woman with twenty-five years of married life behind me. David is graying. Over the years we have both lost *tons* of fat keeping in shape! Our children are almost all adults themselves. Men's eyes no longer turn my way when I walk into a room, they turn my daughter's way—and the wedding discussions in our family center in the hopes, dreams, and desires of my offspring.

But when I go to church, staid and contained, properly garmented and composed on the outside, when I bow quietly in prayer, bending my knees to touch the kneeling pad before me, when I bend in somber silence amid the company of fellow worshipers, I'm dancing within. I'm dancing. Inside, I'm a barefoot bride, clad in the eyeleted lace, the tucked fabric of festal bridal wear, with white ribbons in my hair. I lift my heart in song to the hymns of the church, but I can hear in the far-off distance the beat of a wedding drum, the sound of the tambourine. The young men are gathering by the gate at the Father's house, with laughter and low voices and minstrels, my Lord the tallest among them. The processional is forming.

My hand trembles as it takes the cup—*He is near.* The wedding chamber is being made ready. I am suddenly warmed with the thought of this spiritual intimacy, this rest ahead, that we only taste now.

I have bathed, perfumed myself, become ceremonially clean. The betrothal ring shines golden around my heart. I return to my place in the hard pew, among these friends, their heads bowed, the choir singing, the light filtering through the stained-glass windows, the church bell beginning to call.

I am quiet again, composed, serene. The sound of the wedding drum has faded. And we leave, nodding to acquaintances, shake the hands of our pastors, smile, speak kind words.

But inside, I am still dancing, dancing.

I hear him speak my name in whispers.

But one day the very heavens will break with his shout, *Beloved!*

And I will be ready to answer as though I were the only one.